HIS
Mysterious
WAYS

VOLUME II

HIS
Mysterious
WAYS

VOLUME II

COMPILED BY THE

Editors

GUIDEPOSTS®

Carmel, New York 10512

His Mysterious Ways, Volume II

Book design by Holly Johnson
Cover art by Ed Acuna
Printed in the United States of America

Contents

Preface

Years ago when I was a roving editor for *Guideposts* magazine, I
interviewed a lovely, golden-haired teenager who had lived
through a grizzly accident. At twilight on a summer evening,
just after a brief airplane spin with her boyfriend, she had
stepped in the way of the plane's propeller and her right hand
was severed from her body. That shocking moment marked the
beginning of an unusual series of events.

Medical science was then so advanced that severed hands
could be reattached successfully, but only under certain condi-
tions and especially if not too much time had elapsed between
the accident and the surgical operation. In this case it just so
happened that someone ran immediately to a nearby phone to
telephone the fire department, which just happened to be across
the street from the airfield. Not only did the firemen respond
quickly, but they came prepared with the proper equipment for
carrying the severed hand. It just so happened that at the
hospital, where many staff physicians were away on vacation, a
surgeon with experience in the techniques of such a delicate
operation was moonlighting in the emergency room. And happily, it just so happened that the operation he performed was
brilliantly accomplished, so much so that when I later had
dinner with the young victim and her family, she was able to
handle knife and fork with *both* hands.

At that same dinner with this family whose faith in God was
obviously deep and strong, we reviewed the details of the
accident. "What an amazing series of coincidences," I exclaimed. The mother paused, looked across the table, and said
something to me that I've never forgotten.

"Coincidences?" she said. "There are no coincidences."

Indeed. That is something to think about as you read the
stories collected in this book. All of them are true and most of
them have appeared first in the pages of *Guideposts*. Many of
them, such as Dr. Ritchie's "Return from Tomorrow" and
Professor Harlow's "The Day We Saw the Angels," were published years, sometimes decades ago, yet *Guideposts* subscribers
are constantly requesting us to reprint them. I believe I know
why. It's because they bring us to the core of faith—mystery.
"If the work of God could be comprehended by reason," wrote a

sixth-century saint, "it would no longer be wonderful." These stories stir the wonder in us.

Do things happen by mere chance or by divine design? If our Heavenly Father is watching over us, why does He find it necessary to move in such mysterious ways? I believe you will find your own reassuring spiritual answers in these selections that are—literally—awe-inspiring.

Van Varner, Editor
Guideposts *Magazine*

HIS

Mysterious

WAYS

VOLUME II

HE

Directs

OUR PATHS

Trust in the Lord with all thine heart. . . . In all thy ways acknowledge him, and he shall direct thy paths.

—PROVERBS 3:5–6

GOD'S PLANS
—Author Unknown

> He will silently plan for thee;
> His purposes shall all unfold.
> The tangled skein shall shine at last,
> A masterpiece of skill untold.
>
> He will silently plan for thee,
> Happy child of a Father's care,
> As though no other claimed His love,
> But thou alone to Him wert dear.

THE SECURITY GUARD
Dorothy Nicholas

We were sitting at the table in our Florida home and talking to our next-door neighbors. This young couple had helped us a lot in the past year and a half, after my stroke and my husband's leg injury.

Unexpectedly, the husband began telling us the story of his troubled past. At age sixteen he'd fallen in with the wrong crowd in his hometown of Greenwood, South Carolina, and had spent a year in a reformatory. When he was released he'd had good intentions, but because of his record, he couldn't find a job.

He became desperate and decided to rob a local service station so he could have enough money to leave the state. He stole his father's car and gun and just before closing time drove up to the service window of a gasoline station. He was about to demand all the money from the woman manager.

"But just then," he explained, "I looked up and saw the sign overhead. It read, 'GOD IS OUR SECURITY GUARD—ALWAYS ON THE JOB.' And I knew I couldn't rob that place. I then rushed home and prayed all night. I was determined to get my life straightened out. And with God's help, I did."

As he finished, I looked at my husband. Both of us remembered a night thirteen years ago when I sat at our kitchen table in the same town of Greenwood, South Carolina, trying to make a sign for our business. I had scribbled down several words. Then finally it came, the slogan that my husband put on the sign that stood on the roof of the small service station that we managed:

GOD IS OUR SECURITY GUARD—ALWAYS ON THE JOB.

 ## THE THIF
Jo Hart

After years of wandering, Clint Dennis had come to that point in his life when he knew he had been missing something important. And for months he had felt he could find what that something was in that church on the hillside in North Phoenix.

He arrived at Phoenix First Assembly of God on an unusual day. The choir room was filled with members putting on long robes, tying ropes around their waists, wrapping headdresses around their heads. "Come be part of the mob," a stranger told him.

It was Palm Sunday and the church was reenacting the Crucifixion in costume. Like others in the congregation, he would be part of the crowd that yelled, "Crucify Him! Crucify Him!" Hesitantly he agreed.

Then another stranger hurried up to him. "The man who was supposed to play one of the thieves on the cross didn't show up," he said. "Would you take his place?"

Again he agreed and was shown to the cross where he would look on as Christ died. Just then, though, something about Clint's manner caught a member's eye. He turned to Clint and asked, "Have you ever asked Jesus to forgive your sins?"

"No," Clint replied softly, "but that's why I came here." There beneath the cross, they prayed, and Clint asked Jesus to come into his heart. His life was transformed.

What the church didn't know then was that Clint had been in prison for ten years. Even after his release he had gone on stealing cars and trucks until he knew he had been missing something in life. He was a real thief, but at last he was welcomed into God's kingdom by the same Jesus who welcomed another thief two thousand years ago.

A THING OF BEAUTY
Kenneth Lynch

Years ago, before I moved my metalworking to Connecticut, I had a shop on the West Side of Manhattan—any farther west and you'd get your feet wet. One day an elderly woman came in. When she asked if we could make a chalice for her, I was ready to shake my head.

In the first place, judging from her threadbare coat and her work-gnarled hands, I felt sure she couldn't afford such a costly piece. Such works, as used in serving Holy Communion, are usually handcrafted out of silver and plated with gold. And I didn't have the heart to tell her how much one would cost.

But then, the Gaelic lilt in her voice reminded me of my own great aunt from Ireland. And when she explained that as the mother of a large family, all now grown and dispersed, she wanted the chalice as a gift for her youngest son, shortly to be ordained as a priest, my heart melted.

"How much . . . ?" she ventured. "How much would ye say such a thing would cost?" Reaching inside her coat she withdrew a roll of worn one-dollar bills.

"I've saved through the years for this," she said, lifting her chin a bit, "and I have eighty-five dollars. Will it be enough?"

I was in a dilemma. The bottom price for a handwrought chalice in those days was $150. But she was so hopeful.

"We can do it for seventy-five dollars," I said.

Her eyes lighted up and she pressed all the bills on me. "Take it all," she said, "and make it twice as good. Nothing will be too fine for my youngest on his great day."

"We'll do our best," I promised.

As she walked out of the shop, I turned to see one of our silversmiths who had been standing in the back watching us.

This man was a fine craftsman. He had come to America from Ireland but had learned his art in France. When he worked he was superb, but he couldn't stay away from the bottle. Things had come to the point that I knew I would have to let him go, but now, seeing him, I had a strange feeling that I must give him this one last job.

Calling him up, I told him what the woman wanted and in a meaningful way added, "Now do the best you can."

He nodded and went to his bench.

I prayed that he'd stick to his work and have the chalice ready in time.

The Lord heard my prayer, for the silversmith worked hard on it, often until late at night. There were no more days when he'd phone in "sick" or be in such poor control of himself that I couldn't trust him to forge a hinge. I was surprised at the change in him, and when I'd compliment him on the job he was doing, he'd only give a quick nod and go on with his work.

The chalice was finished—on time—and the silversmith brought it to me for my approval. He stood before me straight and proud. His eyes were clear and forthright as he held up the cup, beautifully wrought in gold-plated silver.

"Well done!" I said enthusiastically. "Well done."

He then went out and bought a handsome case of polished walnut. He lined it himself with fine deep-blue velvet and placed the chalice inside.

When the old woman returned, I presented her with the case. She lifted the lid and gasped.

"Oh . . . oh, it is so beautiful . . . so beautiful!" Then she looked up questioningly. "Are you sure, Mr. Lynch, that eighty-five dollars is enough?"

"Of course, Mother," I said, patting her shoulder. And I meant it. She left the shop thanking "the mighty Lord."

Unfortunately the silversmith wasn't in the shop at the time, but when he came in later, I told him how pleased she had been. "That was a wonderful thing you did," I said, taking his hand. "You made a woman very, very happy."

He looked at me for a moment. "It was something I had to do, Mr. Lynch," he said finally. "You see, that woman—she is my mother."

"But why didn't you—?"

"I've thrown my life away, Mr. Lynch. You know that as well

as I do. When I was a boy I ran away to sea. Never once did I write home. Now I didn't want my mother to see the drunk her son has become. It's better this way . . . until I can be sure of myself."

The next day the silversmith quickly packed his few belongings and left the shop. I never saw him again. But I feel in my heart that he went on to do well. For the mother's love for one of her sons touched the life of another in a way she could never have imagined.

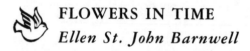

FLOWERS IN TIME
Ellen St. John Barnwell

"Speak to me, Lord, and speak through me." It was my daily prayer and I said it that Sunday at St. Luke's. On the altar, red roses glowed, roses I'd provided in memory of my mother. When the service was over, I turned to my son, Bob. "After we have dinner, let's take the altar flowers to Miss Marie."

"Good idea," he agreed. Mother and Miss Marie, now in her eighties, had been close friends.

Driving home, humming the recessional hymn together, we broke off at the same moment. "Let's take the flowers to Miss Marie right now." The identical thought had occurred to both of us.

"What made you change your mind?" I asked as Bob turned the car toward Miss Marie's house.

"I don't know," was all he could say.

"I don't either." I hesitated. "But let's not waste any time."

Miss Marie's daughter, Alice, answered the doorbell. "How nice!" she said as I handed her the roses. "I've been in bed with the flu." She gestured vaguely. "Mother was resting in her room. Let me see if she's awake now."

Then, a sharp cry.

Bob and I raced down the hall. Miss Marie lay unconscious on the floor. Bob lifted her to her bed. I dialed the emergency ambulance. Alice began sponging Miss Marie's forehead with cool water. Her eyes fluttered.

"Lucky you got to her in time," the medic told us. "When it's a little stroke they can't call for help."

"Couldn't speak," Miss Marie murmured. "Prayed to God in my heart."

That made two prayers He'd answered loud and clear.

 ## PRAYER FOR TOMORROW
—*Carlene A. Wallace*

> Beyond today will be tomorrow,
> But what it will bring of joy or sorrow
> I cannot know. I only pray
> Your guidance, Lord, each hour, each day,
> Your strength to bear whatever may be
> Your loving wisdom has for me.
> So sweet or bitter, sad or gay,
> Be with me, Lord, beyond today.

 ## THE COLUMN OF SMOKE
Joseph Caldwell

I was waiting for the bus to take me down from the Janiculum Hill into the city of Rome when I turned and saw black smoke rising into the sky. It seemed to be coming from my studio, a small, cabinlike study built up against the ancient Roman wall that bounded the grounds of the American Academy. I'd arrived there three weeks before with my most precious possession: the first draft of my new novel.

The smoke—I thought of the electric coil I'd been using to heat water for the endless cups of tea I need to fuel my writing. What if I had started heating water and forgotten. Suppose the coil had slipped from the cup and started a fire that would not only destroy the studio committed to my care for a year but the pages and pages of work I could never duplicate.

I hurried back, but soon saw that the smoke came from a bonfire in the adjoining orchard. I felt relieved, and even a little foolish. But since I was now so close, I went into my studio anyway.

The electric coil *was* still plugged in, and the water I'd meant to use for tea before I left had all boiled out of a cup that had tipped over—and the red-hot coil had toppled onto the desk and was charring the wood. Manuscript pages that would have flared up in a second were only inches away.

Drawn by that column of smoke, I'd come back just in time. "Thank God," I said.

Of course, thank God.

 ## THE WHISTLE
Kerri Tillquist

I was packing that morning when I heard a shrill whistle. I rushed into the living room only to discover it came from the TV. We were preparing to go from Boulder to Montrose, Colorado, with our ten-week-old baby, Leslie.

As we drove through the mountains that afternoon, big sleety drops of rain turned into heavy wet flakes of snow. Near the top of Fremont Pass, traffic slowed and we could barely see. I nursed Leslie and then Neil pulled over and held her. "Is something wrong?" I asked when Leslie's cry suddenly became low and husky.

Neil handed her back to me in a panic. She was coughing and gasping. I patted her on the back, but she turned bluish gray and seemed to stop breathing. I began to administer mouth-to-mouth resuscitation, but without oxygen she could go into respiratory arrest. "Lord," I prayed, "save my baby."

Just then the shrill sound of a whistle pierced the swirling snow. "That's a mine over there," I called to Neil. "Someone will have oxygen there."

Neil started the car and crossed the road to the gate of a molybdenum mine. We flagged a guard, told him our problem, then raced down the drive, where two nurses met us with an oxygen tank. I put the huge mask over Leslie's ashen face and, slowly, she began breathing again.

Later we went to a hospital, where tests confirmed that Leslie was all right. The doctor there had one question: "How did you know there would be oxygen at the mine?"

The shrill sound I had heard that morning was a mine whistle blowing in an episode of *The Waltons*. I watched just long enough to see a miner revived—with oxygen.

THE SKUNK
Elizabeth Sherrill

It was a rustling in the woods that made me glance out the window beside my word processor. At the edge of the trees I caught sight of a skunk, his black-and-white pattern echoing the dappled light. He seemed to be furiously busy—burrowing maybe? My knowledge of skunks began and ended with that appalling odor.

Next moment, though, the animal emerged from beneath the trees and ran zigzagging across the lawn: plumelike tail, striped back and . . . where his head should have been, a bizarre-looking yellow helmet. As he came closer I saw what the "helmet" was. A six-ounce plastic yogurt container.

The carton struck a rock, and the creature whirled in another direction, only to bump up against our picnic table. For a second he stood still, shaking his head frantically. But the yogurt carton was cone-shaped, the narrow mouth wedged fast about his neck. The skunk charged blindly back into the woods.

I stared after him in dismay. How long since he had forced his head into that carton to reach some bit of food on the bottom? How long had he been running in darkness and terror?

It would be the work of a second for me, I thought, to pull that thing off. But the idea of pursuing a skunk through the undergrowth kept me immobilized at the window. How would I ever catch him? And then what? In his panic wouldn't he be certain to spray me?

I sat down and tried to pick up the thread of the story due in the mail that afternoon. But I could think only of an animal running till he dropped from exhaustion. Mustn't this sort of thing have happened before? Might animal experts know what to do?

From the kitchen telephone I dialed the local ASPCA. "We only handle domestic animals," the woman told me. "You want the State Conservation Department." She gave me a number in New Paltz, New York.

New Paltz meant a toll call. Anyhow, by now the skunk would be a long way off. Maybe someone else would see him. Someone braver and more athletic.

I dialed the number in New Paltz. A man in the Department of Wildlife listened to my story, then held a muffled conversation. "As long as skunks can't see you," he said into the phone, "they don't spray."

Well . . . that sounded all right, as long as the skunk's head was inside the container. "What happens after the carton comes off?" I asked.

"Just make sure," the man advised, "that he doesn't feel threatened."

I wondered how one went about reassuring a terrified skunk.

"You could throw a blanket over him," Wildlife suggested. "Then run while he's finding his way out."

"That might work," I said, but I must have sounded as unsure as I felt, because the man asked where I was calling from and began looking up names of conservation officers in my area.

How long would it take, I wondered, for someone to get here? Where would the skunk be by then? Standing there in the kitchen, I was gripped by a sudden strange urgency. I thanked the man, hung up, and ran outside. Without stopping to change out of my next-to-best slacks (*does skunk scent ever wash out?*), and forgetting about the blanket theory, I ran up our driveway to the road.

Of course the skunk wasn't there. Nor did I know why I was. In his frenzy, when I'd seen him last, the animal had been heading the opposite way, straight down the hill into the woods.

But my feet never slowed. I turned left and dashed down the street as though rushing to a long-ordained appointment. I'd run perhaps a hundred yards when a black-and-white streak emerged from the bushes beside the road and ran straight at me, the carton bumping the pavement with each step. I stooped down and grabbed hold of the yogurt carton before the astonishment of finding the skunk hit me.

The animal was tugging and twisting, unexpectedly strong, to get away. *If they can't see you they won't spray.* His front claws scrabbled against the slippery yellow plastic, his body strained backward, and still he could not wrench free of the carton's viselike neck. It took both of my hands tugging the other way to hold on—until a small black head suddenly popped free.

And there we stood, facing each other, two feet apart.

I don't know what *he* saw, and how threatening or not the apparition was, but what *I* saw was a sharp quivering nose, two small round ears, and alert black eyes that stared straight into mine.

For fully ten seconds we held each other's gaze. Then the skunk turned, ran a few yards, and vanished into the mouth of a culvert that runs beneath the road.

For a moment more I stood there, looking after him. Three minutes could not have passed since I hung up the telephone in the kitchen.

But a timeless parable had played itself out, I thought, as I headed back down the drive. The skunk was all those needs I hesitate to get involved in: *Involvement takes time and I have deadlines to meet. I probably can't do anything anyway. Somebody else can handle it better. Besides, involvement can be ugly, and the stench may rub off on me.*

And all these things, of course, may be true. But I've got a yellow pencil-holder on my desk, a rather scratched and battered one, to remind me that every now and then God's answer to a need is me.

MISSION TO THE STRANGEST PLACE
Bruce E. Olson

Looking back on it, I can see how people viewed me as a religious crackpot. I got off the plane in Caracas, Venezuela, that hot August day back in 1962 with only seventy-two dollars in my pocket, nineteen years old, alone, unable to speak Spanish, but convinced that the Lord had told me to go to South America and preach His word to the Indians.

It had all started four years earlier, back in St. Paul, Minnesota, when Jesus Christ became very real to me. My relationship with Him deepened in college, where my aim was to become a professor of languages. However, I began to feel this inner nudge to share His life with those who had never known Him.

"But where, Lord?" I found myself asking.

Then over a period of time, I became interested in South America, particularly Venezuela and Colombia.

I applied to a well-known mission board in Venezuela. They informed me that I didn't have the educational requirements. I was relieved and returned to my dream of becoming a language professor.

Yet God still nudged me.

"But, Lord, I was turned down. I have no contacts, no money, no mission board. You want me to go down there by myself without anyone to take care of me?"

And ever so gently in my mind, the words came, "Bruce, I'm in South America too."

Then came that wonderful feeling of reassurance. Suddenly I knew that with Him by my side I could do anything. But I soon discovered the big difference between plunging ahead on your own power and waiting for His guidance. The Lord knew how inadequate I was. And His preparation came in a series of remarkable incidents.

Soon after I arrived in Caracas, so alone and so ill-equipped, a Venezuelan college student noticed me wandering about the city. We struck up a friendship and I moved into his house where I began to learn the language.

When he learned of my interest in the Indians, he introduced me to a doctor with the government's Indian Commission. Doctor Christian invited me to accompany him by canoe up the muddy Orinoco River. For three weeks I lived with a semi-civilized tribe and learned their ways.

After this trip, the doctor referred me to an American-Venezuelan cultural exchange program in Caracas where I met a man with the Ministry of Health. He asked me to teach English to some university students preparing to attend Harvard University's school of tropical medicine. I did, and at the same time I learned the rudiments of tropical medicine.

One day my superior and I were talking about Indians. "Have you ever heard of the Motilone tribe?" he asked. He described a legendary Stone Age tribe that had resisted civilization since time began. No one had ever learned their language, since few entering their territory ever returned.

These fierce savages, he said, lived in a wild jungle area on the border between Venezuela and Colombia.

Venezuela and Colombia!

I sank back in awe. I knew then that those were the people to whom God wanted me to go.

Within a week I was on a bus headed for the foothills of the Andes Mountains. Then I set off into the jungle alone. Three days later I stumbled half-starved into a settlement of Yucco Indians, a semiprimitive tribe. For eight months I lived with them, learning their language. Finally three Yucco braves reluctantly agreed to take me to a trail that led to the Motilones.

We chopped our way through the jungle for seven days. Suddenly an arrow pierced my thigh. I fell to the ground; my companions fled.

Out of the ferns stepped five squat brown men, eyes glittering under short-cropped hair. I had met the Motilones.

They dragged me to my feet and I limped with them to their settlement. I was thrust into a communal hut where I lay on a palm mat. Days went by; my wound festered. I developed amoebic dysentery and began hemorrhaging blood.

The period that followed was a nightmare of pain and trial. However, I continued to try to bring God's love to those people. Finally, some of them took pity on me and one in particular, a man called Bobarishora, became my friend. As they tried to pronounce my name, "Bruce" became "Bruchko," which has stayed with me ever since.

Meanwhile a powerful chieftain who lived in a distant village heard of me and wanted to kill me. Now I felt impelled to visit this chieftain. If I could gain his friendship, I could travel safely throughout all Motilone territory. My native friends shook their heads but I insisted. However, during the trip to see this chief, I became terribly fatigued.

Suddenly Bobarishora looked at me and gasped, "Bruchko, your eyes have turned yellow!"

I had hepatitis. My only hope was to continue on and trust in God.

The chief was waiting in a frenzy. "Why have you not killed him?"

My friends argued that I was dying already. Later I learned that to a Motilone the worst thing is to die outside your own land. Then your soul is doomed to wander forever.

The chief agreed this would be a fitting end for me. For two weeks I lay in a hut slowly dying. There was little sound except the low murmur of women as they worked.

Suddenly the voices rose in alarm. I heard the distant drone of a helicopter. My friend, Bobarishora, rushed to my side. "Bruchko, the cannibal flute is coming."

The Motilones felt that airplanes were droning flutes of the whiteskins who, they believed, were cannibals who ate Motilones. "Bobby," I pleaded, "carry me out and put a red cloth next to me." He pulled me to a clearing, then fled.

Now I could hear the helicopter land and soon I was looking up into the amazed face of a doctor I had met when I first traveled up the Orinoco River. He explained that he had been visiting an oil company camp. On impulse he asked their pilot to fly him over Motilone territory to take pictures.

I was taken to Maracaibo where I was told it would be six months before I would recover and that I could never return to a jungle climate. But I had a deepening peace in my heart. God had brought me to the Motilones; He would help me to continue. Within three weeks I was back up the river, well supplied with medicines given me by an oil company.

The Motilone chief received me with awe. To him the helicopter had been a sacred vulture sent to take my body. Now I had returned with supernatural prestige. I lived with the Motilones, learning their language, their customs.

But the witch doctors watched me with suspicion. I knew that Motilones believed that evil spirits lived in rocks, trees, and rivers. So one day I placed a smear of river mud under my microscope and showed it to a witch doctor.

"There," I said, referring to the wriggling microbes, "are your evil spirits."

She shrank back in terror. Then I showed her how disinfectant left them lifeless. This is how I first introduced the Motilones to medical science. It was also how their witch doctors became my close allies.

I lived with them for four years, but when I felt ready to give the Motilones the word of God I felt confused and frustrated. They had a vague belief in an entity "who lived somewhere," but where they did not know. Yet how could I introduce God as He really was, independent of my own personality and culture?

I searched for some illustration as a key in introducing the Bible; to them a book was meaningless. I prayed that God would speak through me, that He would show me the right time to do it.

One afternoon the answer came. As Bobarishora, some other men, and I were out walking, we heard agonizing cries echoing through the valley. We looked for their source and found Atabadora, a powerful tribal leader. He had dug a deep pit and was now calling into it for their god to reveal himself. Atabadora's brother had died in a strange territory and he wanted assurance that his brother's spirit would be brought back.

Another man perched in the top of a tall tree was shouting for the great spirit "to come from the horizon." The two had been screaming since sunrise, and as evening shadows crept over them, their voices had dwindled to a croak.

I now found it possible to start a lively discussion. The man in the tree came down and joined us. He reminded us of the tribal legend about the tall man who one day would walk through the tribe carrying a banana stalk out of which God would come.

"Why look for God in a banana stalk?" I asked in puzzlement.

They couldn't explain it. Bobarishora walked over to a banana tree, cut off a cross section, and tossed it to us. "This is the kind of banana stalk our god can come from."

In a mirthful mood, one of the other men struck at the stalk with his machete, hitting it lengthwise.

I gasped.

As it split open, the pale unborn banana leaves unpeeled from within it like the pages of a book.

And now I understood the reason for each step God had had me take in the four years of getting to know the Motilones, of mastering each nuance of their strange and beautiful tongue, of learning how they thought, their hopes and dreams.

I grabbed up my pack and took out my Bible. Flipping open the pages, I pointed to its leaves and said, "This is it. God's language is here. This is God's banana stalk!"

HE

Supplies

OUR NEEDS

But my God shall supply all your need according to his riches in glory by Christ Jesus.

—PHILIPPIANS 4:19

WHAT TO PRAY FOR
—*James A. Bowman*

I asked for bread and got a stone;
I used the stone to grind the grain
That made the flour to form the bread
That I could not obtain.

Instead of asking Him to give
The things for which we pray,
All that we need to ask from God
Is this: show us the way.

SUDDEN INCREASE
Esther McIntosh

I had only two one-dollar bills in my wallet and they had to last until payday, ten days away. My husband was away on business, and I was at home with our two children conserving every cent.

On Monday my father called to say he needed to attend a union meeting on Friday afternoon. Would I come and stay with Mother? She was bedridden with brain cancer and had to have someone help her with her medicine. I didn't hesitate to say yes. Back then, in 1970, one dollar would buy enough gas to get there and back, and I would still have an "emergency" dollar left.

All week long my five-year-old kept asking for a treat from the ice cream truck. And each time, I would open my wallet, show her the two one-dollar bills, and explain why we couldn't afford such a luxury.

When we arrived on Friday, Daddy's parting words were, "Don't forget to give Mom her Dilantin," her anticonvulsant medicine. But after he'd gone I discovered the bottle was empty. I was terrified that if Mother didn't get her medicine on time, she'd go into convulsions.

Mother told me to check her purse and a couple of other places for loose change, but that was all I found—loose change. I telephoned my sisters, but no one was home. The prescription cost over eight dollars. Where would I get that money?

"God will take care of it," Mother said.

At my wit's end, I decided to go to the pharmacist's with my lone dollar and beg him to trust me for the rest. But when I looked in my wallet again, I was stunned.

That single was a ten-dollar bill.

THE LITTLE RED HEN
Josephine M. Kuntz

At one point during the winter of 1940, my husband, a house painter, was temporarily unemployed because of the weather, and the textile plant where I worked was closed due to a seasonal lay-off. We literally had no money. To make matters worse, our eighteen-month-old daughter, Rachel, was recovering poorly from pneumonia, and the doctor insisted we feed her a boiled egg each day. Even that was beyond our means.

"Why not pray for an egg?" suggested our baby-sitter, who was staying on without pay to help us. We were a churchgoing family, but this teenager's depth of faith was something new to us at the time. All the same, she and I got on our knees and told the Lord that Rachel needed an egg each morning. We left the problem in His hands.

About ten o'clock that morning we heard some cackling coming from the hedge fence in front of our house. There among the bare branches sat a fat red hen. We had no idea where she had come from. We just watched in amazement as she laid an egg and then proceeded down the road, out of sight.

The little red hen that first day was a surprise, and we thanked God for it, but can you imagine how startled we were when we heard the hen cackling in the hedge the next morning? And the morning after that, and the morning after that? Every day for over a week, Rachel had a fresh boiled egg.

Rachel grew better and better, and at last the weather turned and my husband went back to work. The next morning I waited by the window and watched. But our prayers had been answered—precisely.

The little red hen did not come back. Ever.

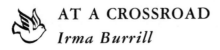

AT A CROSSROAD
Irma Burrill

I couldn't bear the thought of leaving California. After twenty-two years of being moved all around the country, I felt we'd found a home in Merced. Now my husband, Chuck, had retired from the Air Force and was planning to settle us back in Illinois, where we'd both grown up. He felt we should be near our families. I felt we'd put down new roots right where we were; our home, our church, and our friends were in California.

For weeks I had been struggling with the decision as I ferried children about in my job as an elementary school bus driver. That was another thing: I loved my job, I loved the kids, and I even loved the big yellow school bus. So, as the final day of school drew near, I began to wish I hadn't agreed to move, and I pleaded with God: "Please change Chuck's mind."

But Chuck's mind was made up. And before I knew it, the last day of school arrived—my last day as a bus driver.

"Well, this is it, Lord," I whispered that afternoon as I prepared for the routine safety check. I slipped the rubber mallet out of its boot and gave the old bus an affectionate pat on the side as I circled around, thumping each of the tires to check for proper inflation. Then I climbed onto the driver's seat, ready to pick up the kids for the last time.

And all the while I prayed, "Lord, I still don't want to leave all this, but You haven't told me what You want."

So far He hadn't answered.

As I sat waiting for school to let out, I kept mulling over all the reasons for staying. Our three boys had so taken to life in California. They had paper routes, girlfriends, a pet desert tortoise. I thought of the good times we'd had overhauling motorcycles on the living room carpet and sleeping on the roof of our station wagon to study the stars.

The people at church were like family. The church nursery had been my second home for several years, and the Bible study I was in seemed tailor-made for me. And Chuck, why, he was a trustee, a deacon, an usher—he'd even helped put a roof on the church.

"Bus driver," came a child's timid voice, "would you like some candy?" I looked down to see a grubby hand shoving a dripping glob of melted chocolate toward me. I gulped. I'd learned a long time ago that to refuse would be to break a little one's heart.

"Thank you, Maria," I said, smiling as I scooped up the brown mass from the grimy palm. Her face beamed as I poured it into my mouth.

How I loved these little guys and gals, with their jars of caterpillars and ladybugs, the limp roses and half-eaten apples, the hugs, the tears, the nosebleeds, the "Tie my shoe" and "Gee, bus driver, you're older'n my dad!"

As I drove down Bear Creek Drive, I thought of the many times I'd asked God to lift my spirits and He'd sent a covey of baby quail scurrying across the highway, or some kit foxes romping on the hills.

I dropped off the last little guy and watched him wave goodbye to me, appearing as downcast as I was. I swallowed hard and shifted into gear. "I know how you feel, little guy," I sighed.

Back at my reserved space in the bus barn, I switched off the engine and sat for a long moment in the driver's seat, fighting back tears. I had to get it over with. I made my last entry in the log book, then picked up the broom and cleaning cloth from the storage chest under the rear seat.

One by one I turned up the seat cushions, picked up debris, and wiped the seats clean as I worked my way toward the front of the bus. But all the while, I kept wondering why God had seemed so silent to me. I thought He *always* answered prayer.

I stooped to pick up a scrap of cardboard, a piece of a jigsaw puzzle that had fallen face down on the floor. *What good is a puzzle with a piece missing?* I mused.

Then I turned it over and caught my breath. Even in the ninety-degree heat I felt goose bumps springing up all over my body. My downcast spirit began to revive. How could I have doubted? God had answered my prayer after all.

For there in the palm of my hand lay a tiny map of the state of Illinois.

 MORELS IN THE GARDEN
Sandra Fischer

That spring, for the first time in years, Mother couldn't go mushrooming. After surgery, she was recuperating at our home. No scurrying off to the moist Hoosier woodlands. No hunting for morels, the rare coneshaped mushrooms that grow for a short time every spring.

For Mother that was a real hardship; mushrooming was her gift. Every year we kids would go into the woods with her; we'd fan out in different directions, searching in proven morel breeding grounds such as patches of mayapple, rotting stumps, and fallen elm trees. But it was always Mother who would call out suddenly, "Come quick! Look what I've found." And there, in an unpromising pile of decaying leaves, half-hidden, would be the precious honeycomb spikes of morels we'd been seeking.

"These mushrooms are like the manna that God sent the children of Israel in the wilderness," Mother would say. "He chooses when and where He wants them to appear."

That spring, Mother longed to go again to the woods where the morels grew, but forced to stay near home, she puttered listlessly in the garden.

Then one Saturday, Mother was watering the tulips outside the living room window when I heard her cry, "Come quick! Look what I've found."

There among the yellow tulips I spotted something familiar —a cone-shaped morel. We scanned the ground to find another one, and another, growing where they never had grown before —and never have since.

A RIFLE AND A SOLDIER'S PRAYER

Adolf Zinsser, as told to John and Elizabeth Sherrill

I was barely six years old when the conversation around our dining room table began to revolve around a man named Adolf Hitler. Dinner came in the middle of the day, and there were always fifteen to twenty people present, including workmen from the water-powered flour mill that had been in our family for six generations. I can see them now, trooping in from work, still white with flour even after a scrubbing.

The talk about Hitler didn't start right away. First came Scripture reading and prayer. But when the Bible was put on the sideboard and the covers came off the steaming tureens, the excited discussions would begin. Times had been hard in Germany for many years. But Hitler was going to change all that, the grown-ups said. His latest radio address would be discussed point by point.

Papa noted that when Hitler talked about his plans, he would always add, ". . . insofar as the Almighty will help us." It was always *the Almighty,* never *God,* but still . . . "He sounds like a believer," Mama agreed.

Later, of course, Hitler's true colors came out. He began an unstated campaign against any loyalty other than to himself—especially among the young. At the age of ten I had to start attending *Jungvolk* meetings; these "happened" to be scheduled on Sunday mornings, right at church time. At fourteen I graduated to the Hitler Youth. Sunday after Sunday I'd put on my brown shirt and get on my bike and pedal off to march and sing and swear undying allegiance to the Führer.

My parents said little to me about their misgivings—to do so would put us all in danger. Occasionally, though, their feelings would show through. By this time every business letter had to close with the words *Heil Hitler.* One day my father and I were alone in the mill office as he went through his mail. "In this family," he burst out suddenly, "we don't say 'Heil Hitler!' We say, 'Heil Jesus!' "

But though they seldom put their feelings into words, my parents' actions spoke for them. Every Sunday evening a group met for worship in our home. One day the police arrived to

enforce a new law closing such independent churches and confis-
cating their property. They carted away the hymn books, the
portable pulpit, the banner saying "Jesus is Lord," even the
broom Mama used to get the room ready for the meeting.

"The Führer is not against religion," the police chief read
from the new regulations. "You may continue to meet, but
never in groups of more than three."

My father and mother did not hesitate. They shifted the now-
illegal worship services to the mill, where the roar of the water
and the clank of machinery drowned out the songs and prayers.

I was fifteen years old now and tall for my age, blond and
blue-eyed, the very type Hitler associated with his fantasies of a
"master race"—and the kind he wanted for his elite SS. Sure
enough, one day an SS team arrived in our small town of
Plüderhausen, seeking recruits. A dozen of us boys were driven
to a nearby castle, where we were met by an SS officer, splendid
in gleaming boots, braided epaulets, and soft-crowned cap. He
set our pulses pounding as he described the glorious exploits of
his unit in the liberation of neighboring lands. Stressing the
honor being done us, he urged us to enlist then and there.

However, I did not understand the resistance rising within
me. To a youngster of fifteen brought up on Nazi doctrine, as
sensitive to peer pressure as any teenager, everything this dashing hero-figure said seemed undeniable. Yet I felt a need for
caution. Was it my parents' prayers? Again they said little—
but I knew they prayed for me every day. And in the secret
church meeting in the mill, we sang that "prayer removes
mountains."

I refused to volunteer. The officer told me I did not love my
country and called me a coward. I knew the first was not true
and I hoped the second was not true. But still I would not join
the SS.

Two years passed, years of growing loneliness. I was seventeen, enrolled in millers' school, when in the spring of 1944,
along with other teenagers and men too infirm to have been
called up before, I was drafted into the army. The fact that the
military was making do with such unpromising material would
have alerted wiser heads to the fact that Hitler's Thousand-Year
Reich was in trouble. But our radio and newspapers carried only
accounts of victory.

My first night in basic-training camp, the other draftees rode me when I brought out my Bible. "You're crazy," one boy mocked. "That's just the Jews' book of lies. In a few years no one will read it anymore. We'll all be reading *Mein Kampf.*"

From then on, when I wanted to talk to God, I'd go out into the fields, or find an empty storeroom, or pull the blanket over my head at night. Maybe the SS officer had been right when he called me a coward.

At the camp, we were taught to shoot. Our rifles, the sergeant told us, would be everything to us. He warned us never, never to lose the ones we were about to be issued. Anyone who did would be court-martialed. Only after this speech did he hand out our rifles, writing down the serial number in the *Soldbuch* that every soldier had to carry.

To my great surprise I turned out to be an excellent shot. When the instructor collected the paper targets from the firing range, mine would always have the highest score. I was tremendously proud. It wasn't until one night during my prayer time that I began to think about the purpose of all this practice. Suppose that were not a piece of paper in the sights of my rifle, but a man . . .

I thought about my father and mother and their remnant church—mostly women and old men now—meeting three times a week in the noisy mill, risking arrest, which had already happened to some of our Christian friends. "Lord Jesus," I prayed beneath my blanket, "let me never kill a man for a government that makes people hide to worship You."

In May 1944, after a mere two weeks of training, we raw recruits were sent to the French coast to help man Hitler's "impregnable" Atlantic wall. My unit was assigned to a bunker in Normandy, just east of the River Seine. We had been told that our air force would support us if the Allies were so foolish as to attempt an invasion. But although Allied planes flew overhead often, we saw no German ones.

In early June the Allied bombing raids increased. On the night of June 5 the sky throbbed with more planes than I dreamed existed. Toward morning we saw shell flashes in the distance and realized there must be ships offshore. By daylight the rumors were confirmed: the "impossible" invasion had begun.

Our sector was not hit in the initial assault, and our confidence remained high. Each night we climbed out of the bunker and stood scanning the skies. Surely this was the time when the Führer would launch his Secret Weapon!

In mid-June we left the coast and began a tactical maneuver back up the Seine. Not a retreat, our officers stressed—a strategic repositioning for the counteroffensive the Führer would soon be mounting. Now that we were billeted on French farms rather than in fortified bunkers, our wariness over our rifles increased. Each night we placed them beneath the straw we used for beds—each man sleeping on top of his weapon.

Although the din of battle was all around us, our unit had so far done no fighting. Across the Seine, as we moved upriver, we occasionally caught sight of a gray-green tank with a white star on the side. Americans. Once we saw German soldiers struggling toward us across the river, some paddling inflated rafts, others swimming, weapons abandoned. Why didn't Hitler unloose the Secret Weapon?

And then one day tanks opened fire at us from across the river. We scrambled into the fields. I crouched in some waist-high wheat, ran through an apple orchard, stumbled past an area marked LAND MINES, and ran some more.

That night, I joined a unit made up of men from other scattered companies. From then on I moved with such makeshift groups, stopping at a farmhouse for a night or a week, sleeping on my rifle. Although I had now been fired at a number of times, no unit that I'd been with had yet been in a position to return the fire. Was God answering my prayer that I never shoot at a human being?

One night we bedded down in a great stone barn with sentries posted outside. I shaped a pallet of straw, placed my rifle beneath it as usual, and lay down, as always, right on top. Next morning when the corporal roused us we groped under the straw to retrieve our rifles, then lined up stiffly for inspection.

Except me. I was still on hands and knees sifting through my little heap of straw.

"On your feet, soldier!" the corporal barked. "With your rifle!" he snapped as I obeyed.

"I—it—" I stammered. "It's not here!"

"What do you mean, 'not here'?"

I gestured helplessly at the scattered straw. "It was there last night, right underneath me. Only—now it's not."

The entire unit searched that barn from end to end. Those who'd slept nearest me confirmed that I'd placed the weapon where I said. The corporal checked every rifle in the barn against the number in my *Soldbuch*. No other soldier had taken it—and no one from outside could have got in past the guards. How could a rifle disappear into thin air?

The corporal was fuming. Our orders were to march out, and I'd delayed us all! Nor was there a spare rifle to give me. Our troops were short of everything—ammunition, weapons, medicine. All that day we marched, followed by our horse-drawn supply cart, while I saw myself standing in front of a firing squad, my parents getting the news . . .

Late that same afternoon we engaged in our first exchange of fire. The Allies were on the other side of a small valley. Our squad took cover and began firing. Except me. With no rifle to shoot, I was put in charge of the terrified horse. As bullets whined around us I tried to calm the panicky animal, though I was easily as frightened as he.

It wasn't until that night, reading my Bible in a solitary corner of yet another barn, that I realized what had happened. That day, for the first time, the order had come to shoot. That day, for the first time, I had been unable to obey.

For the next several days I marched and bivouacked and carried equipment, but I never fired a weapon because I did not have one. The threat of court-martial hung heavy over me, but we were regrouping too often for official procedures to be followed through.

One morning in July my current unit was approaching a bridge when two Canadians armed with submachine guns jumped up on either side of the road.

"Halt! Hands up!"

Our lieutenant had an automatic pistol, which he let drop as he raised his hands. The rest of us threw our rifles clattering to the ground. All, of course, except me.

The mystery of the missing rifle was never solved. I spent the final ten months of the war as a prisoner in England, working on a farm owned by a family that reminded me a lot of my own. I worried about my parents, of course, as the Allied forces pushed on into Germany and the fighting drew near to Plüderhausen. All I could do was pray that they be kept safe (and they were!), as they had prayed for me.

Praying was a lot, though. That was a truth I learned at age seventeen, groping about in some straw on a stone floor. Prayer can indeed remove mountains— and rifles too.

WHEN THE LIGHTS CAME ON
Franklin Graham

In 1971, as a newly licensed pilot, I was flying with my flight instructor from Vero Beach, Florida, to Longview, Texas. That night, we hit bad weather over Mobile, Alabama, and air-traffic controllers suggested we fly north toward Jackson, Mississippi, to avoid an approaching storm.

As we rose above the clouds, I noticed the instrument panel lights flicker. A minute later, radios and instruments started going dead; then all our lights went out. Our situation was desperate, and as we flew an emergency triangle, we prayed to God for His protection. We decided to drop below the clouds and try to see the ground. Soon we spotted the distant lights of Jackson and headed for the airport's rotating beacon.

We circled the control tower twice, then got a green light to land. Without any electrical power, we had to lower the landing gear manually. At that moment, all the strobe landing lights came on and slowly, safely we touched ground.

Then the landing lights went off. *That's odd,* I thought, *at least they could have waited until we taxied to the ramp.* It was even odder when a man from the tower asked us, "Who gave you permission to land?"

And then, little by little, we learned that no one in the tower had seen us circling overhead. The green light had been flashed by a traffic controller who was explaining to his visiting pastor what he would do in case a plane ever attempted to land without radio communication. The emergency landing lights were part of the same demonstration.

But the whole story can never be explained—just accepted with gratitude, as I strive to serve the Lord each new day.

A STRANGE PLACE TO HOPE
Corrie Ten Boom

Rank upon rank we stood that hot September morning in 1944, more than a thousand women lining the railroad siding, one unspoken thought among us: *Not Germany!*

Beside me my sister Betsie swayed. I was fifty-two, Betsie fifty-nine. These eight months in a concentration camp since we had been caught concealing Jews in our home had been harder on her. But prisoners though we were, at least till now we had remained in Holland. And now when liberation must come any day, where were they taking us?

Behind us guards were shouting, prodding us with their guns. Instinctively my hand went to the string around my neck. From it, hanging down my back between my shoulder blades, was the small cloth bag that held our Bible, that forbidden book which had not only sustained Betsie and me throughout these months, but given us strength to share with our fellow prisoners. So far we had kept it hidden. But if we should go to Germany . . . We had heard tales of the prison inspections there.

A long line of empty boxcars was rolling slowly past. Now it clanged to a halt and a gaping freight door loomed in front of us. I helped Betsie over the steep side. The dark boxcar grew quickly crowded. We were pressed against the wall. It was a small European freight car, thirty or forty people jammed it. And still the guards drove women in, pushing, jabbing with their guns. It was only when eighty women were packed inside that the heavy door slid shut and we heard the iron bolts driven into place outside.

Women were sobbing and many fainted, although in the tight-wedged crowd they remained upright. The sun beat down on the motionless train, the temperature in the packed car rose. It was hours before the train gave a sudden lurch and began to move. Almost at once it stopped again, then again crawled forward. The rest of that day and all night long it was the same, stopping, starting, slamming, jerking. Once through a slit in the side of the car I saw trainmen carrying a length of twisted rail. Maybe the tracks ahead were destroyed. Maybe we would still be in Holland when liberation came.

But at dawn we rolled through the Dutch border town of Emmerich. We were in Germany.

For two more incredible days and two more nights we were carried deeper and deeper into the land of our fears. Worse than the crush of bodies and the filth was the thirst. Two or three times when the train was stopped the door was slid open a few inches and a pail of water passed in. But we had become animals, incapable of plan. Those near the door got it all.

At last, on the morning of the fourth day, the door was hauled open its full width. Only a few very young soldiers were there to order us out and march us off. No more were needed. We could scarcely walk, let alone resist. From the crest of a small hill we saw it, the end of our journey, a vast gray barracks city surrounded by double concrete walls.

"Ravensbrück!"

Like a whispered curse, the word passed back through the line. This was the notorious women's death camp itself, the very symbol to Dutch hearts of all that was evil. As we stumbled down the hill, I felt the Bible bumping on my back. As long as we had that, I thought, we could face even hell itself. But how could we conceal it through the inspection I knew lay ahead?

It was the middle of the night when Betsie and I reached the processing barracks. And there under the harsh ceiling lights we saw a dismaying sight. As each woman reached the head of the line she had to strip off every scrap of clothes, throw them all onto a pile guarded by soldiers, and walk naked past the scrutiny of a dozen guards into the shower room. Coming out of the shower room, she wore only the thin regulation prison dress and a pair of shoes.

Our Bible! How could we take it past so many watchful eyes?

"Oh, Betsie!" I began—and then stopped at the sight of her pain-whitened face. As a guard strode by I begged him in German to show us the toilets. He jerked his head in the direction of the shower room. "Use the drain holes!" he snapped.

Timidly Betsie and I stepped out of line and walked forward to the huge room with its row on row of overhead spigots. It was empty, waiting for the next batch of fifty naked and shivering women.

A few minutes later we would return here stripped of everything we possessed. And then we saw them, stacked in a corner, a pile of old wooden benches crawling with cockroaches, but to us the furniture of heaven itself.

In an instant I had slipped the little bag over my head and stuffed it behind the benches.

And so it was that when we were herded into that room ten minutes later, we were not poor, but rich. Rich in the care of Him who was God even of Ravensbrück.

Of course when I put on the flimsy prison dress, the Bible bulged beneath it. But that was His business, not mine. At the exit, guards were feeling every prisoner, front, back and sides. The woman ahead of me was searched. Behind me, Betsie was searched. They did not touch or even look at me.

Outside the building was a second ordeal, another line of guards examining each prisoner again. I slowed down as I reached them, but the captain shoved me roughly by the shoulder. "Move along! You're holding up the line!"

So Betsie and I came to our barracks at Ravensbrück. Before long we were holding clandestine Bible study groups for an ever-growing group of believers, and Barracks 28 became known throughout the camp as "the crazy place, where they hope."

Yes, hoped, in spite of all that human madness could do. We had learned that a stronger power had the final word, even here.

SNOWFLAKES IN SEPTEMBER
Robert Hawkins

In September last year Sister Grace began forming a picture of a Christmas tree in her mind. As the director of pastoral care at Charleston's St. Francis Xavier Hospital, Sister Grace had been asked to decorate the tree that would be placed in the lobby of the Omni Hotel. The tree would have angels on it and snowflakes—lots of snowflakes, exquisite ones crocheted by hand. By Thanksgiving Sister Grace had acquired the angels, but the snowflakes were not to be found.

On the day before Thanksgiving, Doris Hartvig was admitted to the hospital for tests. Doris detested idleness, and she was soon busy at work with needles and yarn.

"Could you do a snowflake?" one of the nuns, Sister Mary Joseph, asked her.

"I can," Doris replied. In fact, not long ago she had bought a book that described how to crochet snowflakes. They weren't easy to do, and each one required a lot of time.

With renewed hope, Sister Grace went to see Doris. She described in detail the Christmas tree she had her heart set on: a blue bow on top, angels clinging to the branches, and lacy snowflakes hanging from the boughs.

"How many snowflakes do you need?" Doris finally asked. "We should have sixty," Sister Grace replied, "but there's no time to make that many."

Doris smiled. She reached under her bed and took out a bag of needlework, and then drew out one beautiful crocheted snowflake after another—forty, fifty, over sixty of them! They were ironed, starched, and ready to be hung.

In September Doris Hartvig had felt a great urge to crochet snowflakes. Now she knew why.

THE PENNY GIFT
John Sherrill

In 1987 while my wife and I were on a sixteen-month, free-lance writing stint in Europe, I had one more reminder that God does provide, even in unexpected ways. It was the year of the dollar devaluation. Week after week we watched the money we'd brought with us shrink against other currencies. As our cost of living soared, so did my anxiety.

I was at my most anxious one morning when I pulled into a self-service gas station just off one of the autobahns in Germany. The dollar's latest plunge had brought fuel to the equivalent of three dollars a gallon, and I was muttering to myself as I turned on the pump and watched the "amount due" dial spin faster than my eye could follow.

At that moment I noticed a young man ambling up the street in my direction. Wearing stained corduroy trousers and a torn sweater, he had the childlike look that so often goes with mental retardation. He stopped and stood watching me fill the tank.

As I withdrew the nozzle the young man edged closer and at first I thought he wanted a ride. But he had drawn a small purse from his pocket and was fumbling with the clasp. He emptied a few coins into his hand and with clumsy fingers selected one of them.

"Für dich," he said. *For you.* He held out a one-pfennig piece, worth less than half a U.S. cent.

"For me? But I don't need . . ."

I stopped short. In fact I had just been feeling very much in need. I stood there with the gasoline hose in one hand, the little copper in the other, watching God's spokesman wander off up the street.

BECAUSE
—*Inez Franck*

> Because somebody cared today
> I knew God's love was strong;
> I found new hope to bear my cross
> And courage for my song.
> My neighbor's heart conveyed the love
> I needed for my pain;
> And happily I felt the faith
> To dream and smile again.

THERE WAS PLENTY!
Adele Hooker

I've always had a strong faith in God, but I had never looked for miracles in my life. Until a few years ago . . .

When our family of four lived in Muskogee, Oklahoma, our income was so small we could barely pay for necessities. Sometimes it was cornflakes and milk for a week. On one such occasion, friends traveling through town stopped in, and to my amazement, my husband invited them for dinner.

I fidgeted, then went into my bedroom, knelt down, and asked God how I was to cook a dinner with no food in the house.

"But you have," came the answer that formed in my head. "You have meat in the freezer." (I didn't believe it.) "You have vegetables." (Maybe a can of beans.) "Make a stew. And you have flour. Make biscuits." (That I could do. I'm a good biscuit builder.)

I went to the kitchen to prove my inner voice wrong, but there in the freezer lay a small amount of hamburger, in the crisper lay half an onion and a carrot, and in the bin under the sink were two small potatoes.

I made the stew. Hadn't I asked God for help? What could I do but follow the directions that seemed to come to me? I put the flimsy fare in a pot, mixed up the biscuits, then set the table.

When I took up the stew there was barely enough to fill a medium-size serving bowl; I thought my husband and I would eat only biscuits and milk. But when I passed the stew around, behold, there was plenty. I served us and passed the bowl around again!

When our dinner was over, the guests thanked me for the delicious meal. And I gathered up leftovers.

We had *leftovers*. We did, we really did!

HE

Preserves

OUR LIFE

Jehovah himself is caring for you! He . . . preserves your life.

—PSALM 121:1, 7, TLB

COURAGE
—*Paul Gerhardt, translated by John Wesley*

Give to the winds thy fears;
   Hope and be undismayed;
God hears thy sighs and counts thy tears,
   God shall lift up thy head.

Through waves and clouds and storms
   He gently clears thy way;
Wait thou His time; so shall this night
   Soon end in joyous day.

Leave to His sovereign sway
   To choose and to command;
So shalt thou wondering own, His way
   How wise, how strong His hand!

Far, far above thy thought
   His counsel shall appear,
When fully He the work hath wrought
   That caused thy needless fear.

Let us in life, in death,
   Thy steadfast truth declare,
And publish with our latest breath,
   Thy love and guardian care.

THE MISSING SHOES
Elizabeth Sherrill

Of all times to have the airline lose my luggage! It was only my
toiletries case with my one pair of good shoes, but of all places
to wind up without them!

   I'd flown out to Farmington, New Mexico, for a one-day

seminar sponsored by the Southwest Christian Writers' Association. "No one will care about your shoes," Margaret, the group's president, assured me.

Doubtless Margaret was right, but *of all times*. Even as I said it, a phrase came to mind: ". . . we should at all times, and in all places, give thanks unto Thee." At *all* times.

We met at the First Presbyterian Church. At the seminar's close, several writers came up to the speaker's stand. Suddenly there was a terrifying *crack*. Then a woman shouted, "Lie down! Everyone!"

Two men were outside, one of them brandishing a gun. The sound of exploding glass had come from the window. Later we learned that the men had been drinking and shooting at telephone poles. From the wall beyond the speaker's stand the police recovered the tip of an electric screwdriver fired from a homemade pistol.

While Margaret filled out the police report, the rest of us said good-bye, each no doubt recalling a step forward or a delay that had kept him or her out of the line of fire.

For my part, I was tracing a trajectory, from the window to the wall, an inch over the spot where I'd been standing. I was thinking of a pair of two-and-a-half-inch heels in a missing bag, and echoing a prayer: ". . . we should at all times, and in all places, give thanks to Thee, O Lord."

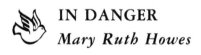

IN DANGER
Mary Ruth Howes

When I was growing up, I always liked to hear my father tell the story of a strange premonition he'd had as a young missionary in China. Dad's superior, a Mr. Sinton, had just left Luchow for an extended journey to outlying missions, when Dad was overwhelmed with the feeling that Mr. Sinton was in mortal danger. Every night, Dad prayed for his safety.

When Mr. Sinton returned, he told about having retired one night in a guest house where a tiny charcoal brazier burned. Later that evening Mr. Sinton had heard a loud mysterious pounding. Getting up, he went to the window, pushed it open, and looked out. No one was there. He started toward the door, but the next thing he knew, he was waking up flat on the floor. He had been overcome by toxic fumes from the brazier. Opening the window had saved his life!

Several years ago, when Dad was eighty-two, he called me at the office. "I had such a vivid dream early this morning," he said, "that I had to call you. I dreamed you were in danger. Is your house okay?"

I didn't want to do it, but remembering Dad and Mr. Sinton, I actually went home—only to discover my sick cat sleeping in front of the electric heater. No fire. No danger. I turned off the heater and, feeling foolish, returned to the office.

At home that night, I turned on the heater again, and fifteen minutes later the lights in the kitchen sizzled and flickered out. The motor on the heater had burned out, blowing the fuses and filling the kitchen with acrid smoke . . .

THE HOLDUP
Steve Akers

It was 9:00 P.M., February 6, 1981—closing time at the self-service Husky Gas Station in Albuquerque, New Mexico, where I'd been employed for about two months. As I counted out the day's receipts and put the money into a bank bag, I thought again how lucky I'd been to get this job. In the two years since I'd graduated from high school, I'd had a hard time finding good, steady work.

My mother, however, had not been pleased when I'd told her about my new job.

"Steve, I'm scared," she'd admitted. "I read all the time about robberies at those self-service stations. What if you get hurt?"

"Don't worry, Mom, I'll be fine," I'd reassured her. "Nothing is going to happen."

Now, looking forward to the dinner waiting for me at home, I slipped my fleece-lined denim jacket over my white T-shirt and blue corduroy pants, tucked the bag under one arm, and left the cashier's booth near the pumps to cross the parking lot to the storage shed where the safe was located. En route, I passed a man wearing a black windbreaker and black pants. He mumbled something to me, but I just nodded and went on. People on foot often cut across that parking lot, so I felt no alarm.

I stashed the money in the safe, then hurried outside and locked the shed. I'd started to turn back toward the booth when the same man I'd seen five minutes before stepped around from behind the shed and stopped me. A shock flashed through me at the sight of the black ski mask he'd pulled down over his face. The thing that turned my knees to Jell-O, though, was the gun he held in his black-gloved hand.

"Oh, my God," I gasped.

"That's right," he responded coolly.

Meaning, I knew, that he was about to hold me up, and he could see that I realized it. He motioned with the gun toward the booth, which was still unlocked and brightly lighted.

"Give me your money," he said.

He hadn't seen that bag under my arm, then. He didn't know I'd locked the money in the shed.

"I don't have any money," I told him.

He snorted in disbelief. "Don't give me that! Get in there and open that cash register!"

I moved toward the booth, trying to control my rubbery legs, which threatened to pitch me forward onto the asphalt.

"I'm telling you the truth," I insisted. "All I've got left are some rolls of change." And then, realizing I'd have to explain that, I did tell a lie: "The manager came by just a while ago and picked up the rest of the money. You're too late."

"Oh yeah? I'll have to see for myself."

He followed me into the booth. I glanced out toward the empty street, usually so busy. Surely someone would drive by and see what was happening, I told myself. All I had to do was try to stay calm until help arrived. Calm? My hands trembled as I groped for the lever on the register. The drawer slid open.

"Look, just change," I told him.

He began to curse. His eyes glared ferociously at me through the holes in the mask. He looked insane. Or high on dope. Still holding the gun on me, he began rummaging through the shelves in the booth with his other hand, hunting for the bag of money he seemed convinced was there.

"Pull the phone off the wall," he told me shortly.

The hole in the barrel of the gun, pointed at my chest, looked as big to me as the hole in the end of a car's tailpipe. I grabbed the phone with both hands and yanked. It didn't budge. I tried again, but my arms had all the strength of wet spaghetti. Finally, I picked up a small knife and cut through the cord.

He's just making sure I won't call the police, I said to myself. *Now he'll leave, and I can go home.*

That's all I wanted right then—just to go home, to the safety of my own four walls, to the love and support of my parents. I'd tell my younger brother about the attempted robbery. He'd be surprised, maybe not even believe me at first. Home . . .

The man peered through the window of the booth toward my 1973 Chevy Impala parked nearby.

"The money must be in your car," he snapped. "Get moving."

And he motioned again with the gun.

We left the booth and walked across the parking lot to the car. He searched me there, looking for rolls of money in my pockets. All he found was my wallet, which he kept. Then he told me to open the car. Still keeping the gun pointed in my direction, he felt around under the empty seats.

"Get in," he demanded. "You drive. Pretty soon I'll have you drop me off somewhere."

I wanted to believe him. After all, I argued to myself, I had nothing to give him. Sooner or later, he'd have to let me go.

We headed down the street in the car. When the man noticed that the gas tank registered almost empty, he went into a rage. He began to taunt me about making minimum wage at a gas station and not being able to afford gas for my own car.

"Look at me, I can get plenty of money any time I want it," he boasted, "and I don't have to work for no crummy minimum wage."

Then he told me that he was the man who had murdered Phil Chacon, a popular Albuquerque policeman who had been shot to death several months before. That murder was still unsolved.

My heart began to pound. My hands, damp with perspiration, slipped on the surface of the steering wheel. For the first time I looked at the fact that this man might kill me.

I needed help. I wanted to reach out to someone, anyone, but only God knew the danger I was in. Somehow my grandmother's face appeared in my mind, smiling at me the way she had when I was little. She'd been the one in our family with a strong belief in God. I'd wanted to believe in God, too—but for me, now as then, He seemed far away, out of reach. I just couldn't get in contact with Him, not the way she could.

Maybe it was because I'd always felt shy and insecure. Despite my parents' encouragement. Despite my grandmother's love. For I'd had some physical problems as a child that had kept me from developing as fast as my friends. While they shot up to become basketball and football stars, I remained slight of build. When they all began talking in deep voices and shaving every morning, I still looked, with my baby face, like a twelve-year-old. I gradually drew away from others at school, staying in my own corner, never speaking up in class. Even though I finally grew to be over six feet tall in my last two years of high school, my habit of staying in the background continued. That's another reason I'd never called on God—I thought someone as unimportant as I was didn't stand a chance of being heard.

Now, with this masked gunman sitting beside me, I *wanted* to be noticed. I kept hoping that someone would glance into our car at an intersection and see what was happening. One man in a car did pull up beside us, but then the light changed, and he took off, leaving me once more alone. Or was I alone?

Desperately, I began to pray: "God, if You're listening, I sure do need help. Maybe I am a nobody—maybe I've never done anything important—but I still don't want to die. Please—please, can You do something?"

The gunman told me what streets to take and where to turn. I saw at last that we were headed toward the airport near the south edge of town.

I said, "Look, I'll just let you out, and I'll go away, and you'll never hear from me again. You've only taken about fifteen dollars in change. I'll make that up out of my own pocket, and no one will ever know . . ."

The old coward bit. I'd fantasized, when I was younger, about all the brave things I'd do if I were ever in a jam. But actually looking into the barrel of a gun had sent my once-imagined courage right down the tubes.

"I haven't decided yet what to do with you. Just keep driving," he told me flatly.

When we came to a fork where the road circled to the left, into a loading area in front of the airport terminal building, the man had me veer instead to the right, down a winding dirt road that led out into the deserted dunes beyond the west end of the runways. In the glow of the headlights, I saw clumps of dead *chimisa* and trash-draped tumbleweeds. The rocky dunes rolled away on either side, bleak as the surface of the moon.

My chest felt constricted. My breathing had become fast and shallow.

"Lord, this really looks bad," I prayed silently. "Are You here? Are You with me?"

At the same time, a part of me kept rationalizing—maybe the man really didn't intend to kill me. Why should he, what would he gain? Maybe he'd just let me out and then steal my car. It would take me a while to get back to the main road where I could flag down a ride. But at least I'd be safe—the nightmare would be over, and I could go home . . .

"Stop," the man suddenly barked.

I pulled over toward the side of the road and turned off the key.

"Now get out. Leave the key in the ignition," he instructed.

I felt greatly relieved. *Good,* I thought, *he'll soon be gone.*

I climbed out and moved a few steps away, into the sand and tumbleweeds. The man slid over and got out too, coming to stand directly in front of me. Without saying another word, he brought the gun up, pointing it at my face.

It's amazing the number of thoughts that can flash through a person's mind in just one split second. I knew that I was going to die right then, and there was nothing I could do. I felt no sorrow for myself, but I grieved for my parents and what they would have to go through, trying to deal with such a terrible memory for the rest of their lives.

Well, Lord, this is it, I thought, becoming strangely calm.

All that, in the brief time it took the man to level the gun and pull the trigger.

I saw the flash, I heard the explosion. I waited to fall. Nothing happened. I stood on my feet, staring straight into the barrel. Had he missed? He couldn't have missed . . .

He pulled the trigger again. Again, I saw the flash and heard the explosion. Again, incredibly, I found myself still on my feet, facing that gun.

It misfired, I thought . . . but in that case, there would just have been a click, no flash or loud noise. Blanks? Even with those, there should have been a blast of some kind, powder burns, at that close range . . .

Where had those bullets gone?

I stared at the man, he stared at me. Then he looked in a puzzled way at the gun. He started to pull the trigger again, but seemed to change his mind. Instead, he taunted me about how close I'd come to death.

"You're lucky this time," he concluded, motioning toward the road. "Start walking."

I took off at once, stumbling through the sand and gravel. I couldn't believe that I was still alive. My mind reeled as I tried to take it in. To have the gun fail once seemed to me to be a miracle. But *twice* . . .

I snapped back to the present with a new shock of alarm, realizing that the car was rocketing up behind me like a race car roaring off the starting line. Before I could dive out of the way, the front bumper slammed into the backs of my legs. The car continued to speed forward as my body catapulted into the air and crashed headfirst onto the hood. With arms and legs flailing, I bounced over the windshield to the top of the car. From somewhere came the sound of breaking glass as my body careened about, somersaulting onto the trunk and then smacking face down into the road.

The car roared off. I lay there, stunned, with sand in my mouth. *But I was still alive!* Broken and helpless, no doubt, but alive . . .

Gingerly, carefully, I began to stir, testing for broken bones. I thought my legs would surely be fractured from the impact of the bumper, or my skull cracked and my neck snapped from the crash onto the hood. But all my joints worked with no trouble. I pushed to my knees, blinking against the sting of gravel in my left eye. Getting my feet under me, I rose to my full height under the brilliant glitter of the desert stars.

Broken bones? Not one! Only a few skinned places on my face and chest, a knot on my head, and the gravel in my eye. I'd been shot at twice and run down with my own car—and there I stood, virtually unhurt.

I heard myself saying aloud, "Thank You, thank You, thank You," over and over. And I knew that I was thanking God. Because to come out whole through three attempts on my life seems to me to be more than just coincidence. I really think the hand of God had to be at work in there somewhere.

I headed through the dunes toward the distant glow of lights in the fifteen-story hotel at the airport. With my clothes torn and dirty, with blood from the skinned places seeping through my T-shirt, I finally stumbled into the lobby and asked the startled desk clerk to phone for the police.

Later, the police and I found my car abandoned near the airport with two blue imprints from my pant legs ground into the bumper, a big dent in the hood where my head had hit, and a broken right window, which I must have kicked with one foot in my tumble over the car. Although the person who kidnapped me was never identified, there was a man of the same height and build convicted a few months later, along with another man, for the murder of policeman Phil Chacon. When I looked at the eyes of that man in a newspaper picture, I felt a shock jar my nerves. He might well have been the man in the ski mask, although I can't say for sure.

But one thing I do know for sure: my old sense of worthlessness is gone. It doesn't matter that I was never a big football star or a straight "A" student—when I called to God, He heard me. To Him, I was not unimportant. Now that my life has been spared, I'm determined to make the most of the talents I do have, whatever they may be.

Because of that resolve, I reported to work on time the day after I'd been kidnapped. The people in charge were impressed by that and soon promoted me, making me the youngest person in the city ever to become a Husky station manager.

I'm pleased by the promotion, of course. But even if that hadn't happened, I know God would still care for me anyway, no matter what I look like or what kind of so-called "crummy" salary I might be drawing.

I haven't yet been able to forgive the man who tried to kill me, but I'm working on it. Meanwhile—with God's help—I have a station to run.

STRANGE DAY AT LAKE MUNKAMBA

William F. Pruitt

1968. Kasai Province, Zaire, Africa. As one of the missionaries who had been allowed to return to his former station in what was once the Belgian Congo, I'd been "itinerating" for several weeks—that is, visiting among the tribal missions in a radius of about a hundred miles of my station in Moma. One evening, after preaching and showing Cecil B. DeMille's 1927 classic film, *King of Kings,* I found that I was only about thirty miles from our house on Lake Munkamba.

Almost on impulse I decided to spend the night there. It was late, after eleven, and I was very tired. But I was also tired of sleeping in my house-truck. Besides, I wanted to see the house again.

This was no ordinary house. I don't mean architecturally, though that too, given the local standards. It was extraordinary because it was *ours*—the only home in Africa that was our very own. We had built it years before as a hideaway for little family vacations, and now, with Virginia and our two sons far away in America, I longed even more to go there. The house represented home and love and a security that often seemed elusive in those days of internal African strife. I needed to be reminded of these qualities once more.

As I drove toward the lake, I wondered in what condition I'd find our hideaway this time. During the tribal fighting of the early 1960s, it had been looted frequently. Doors and windows and most of the furnishings—as well as the much-coveted tin roof—had been carried away. Our roof now covered the local chief's hut, but he had explained his taking it. "When I saw those looters taking everything from your house," he had said, "I knew you would want me instead of them to have that tin roof!" Logic against which I could offer no rebuke.

At last I arrived. The house was still there. I fumbled my way in the darkness through the bare living room to a cot in one of the bedrooms and fell upon it. Exhausted, I was soon asleep.

I awakened early the next morning, looked about a little, and said my prayers. I thanked God for another day of life and asked

Him to watch over me. Outside, through the morning mist, I saw a lone native fisherman on the shore nearby. There seemed to be no one else about. All was quiet. African quiet.

Time to get going, I told myself, and took my five-gallon jerry can to the spring and filled it with drinking water. Back at the house, I picked up my hat, and was about to leave when I caught sight of the fisherman again. It made me wish I had time to join him for a quick catch. *Well, someday,* I thought. *I'd just better check to see if that outboard motor I left last summer is still here.* With so much looting, there was no telling what might have become of a prize like an outboard motor.

I put down the jerry can and went to a small storeroom in the back of the house. It was windowless and gloomy inside, but I could see that the motor was still there. *That's a relief,* I thought, reaching down and patting it as if to say, "Good boy! Stay there, because you and I have some fishing to catch up on as soon as I can get a day off!"

At just that moment I became aware of something else in a corner of the room. It was black and coiled into a circle, as though very carefully placed there. *I don't remember having a rope like that,* I said to myself. I went over to have a closer look. I went *too* close.

Oh! Oh, dear Lord!

Zoom!

I felt a spray of liquid; it was as though a red-hot nail had been driven through my right eye!

Instantly I knew that what I had taken for a coiled rope was a spitting cobra, one of the most poisonous snakes in the world!

I screamed out loud and started running, running away, but I no sooner got to the door than I stumbled over the jerry can of water. Quickly I threw myself down on all fours and frantically splashed cold water into my face, trying to put out the fire that was spreading through my head.

A figure loomed over me. *"Muambi!"** What is the matter?" It was the fisherman from the lake.

He looked at me, looked at the room, and ran away. *He knows what has happened,* I told myself. *He knows there's nothing he can do. He's probably gone to tell the chief that I am here and dying.* Every native African knows that the spitting cobra first blinds and

---

*"Preacher" or "Missionary" in the Tshiluba language.

paralyzes its victim with a deadly venom before attacking again.

The pain was excruciating. Where was the snake now? I went on splashing water on my face even though I knew my flailing might cause it to strike again.

Was I beginning to feel a numbing sensation creeping over me? It seemed that way, but I wasn't sure.

Minutes went by, maybe five, maybe ten. Three people entered the room. Strangers. A man and two women, white.

The man rushed to me. "What's happened?" he asked, and I stuttered out the word, "Cobra."

He ran outside and came back with a large stick. "There it is!" he yelled, as he lifted the stick and again and again brought it down on the snake's head, killing the creature—a seven-foot-long female carrying seven eggs!

One of the women came to me, checked my pulse, and tried to look into my blinded eye. "I'm a nurse," she said. Then she looked up at the other two people helplessly. "I don't know what to do, but I feel I *must* do something!" Then, as almost an afterthought, she opened her handbag and started searching for something. "A sample of an eye medication came to me in the mail the other day. I don't know anything about it," she said, addressing me, "but it's all we have. Shall I try it on you?"

I understood what she was really saying: The poor man is going to die anyway—or go blind; why not take the gamble?

I nodded and she put a few drops of the unknown prescription in my eye.

"It's just possible that the water you threw on your face helped," the nurse said. Now we waited to give the medication time to do its work, if it was going to.

A half hour passed. Just as the pain seemed to be easing, we heard footsteps. Another white man appeared, a stranger to the others. I was mystified. Where were all these people coming from? In those days in that part of Africa, no unidentified white man traveled alone.

Who was he? A French doctor, he said, on his way to a diamond mine fifty miles away. He'd heard of the beautiful Lake Munkamba and he'd detoured several miles off his route, parked his car a half mile away, and walked down to the shore of the lake.

The nurse explained to him what had happened to me. "Do you know how to treat venom in the eye?" she asked.

"Yes," he answered. He told us of an effective new antibiotic. In fact, he had used it successfully on a man at the diamond mine just the month before. Unfortunately, he didn't have any with him.

"Do you know anything about this?" the nurse asked, handing him the medication she had put in my eye.

He looked at it carefully. "That's it! That's it! That's the very one I was telling you about!"

The French doctor stayed for a while. Then, after giving instructions for applying the drops every thirty minutes and telling me to stay in bed for the next twenty-four hours, he left us, as quickly and mysteriously as he had arrived. None of us had even learned his name!

Now, however, I learned who my other saviors were: a Scottish missionary and his wife who were vacationing nearby and a nurse visiting them from an English mission. The kindly Scotsman took me to his house and put me to bed.

The next morning my eyesight was fully restored, my energy had returned, and my eye was not even red! Today I see as well from one eye as from the other.

But for the rest of that long day, and throughout the longer dark hours of the night, I lay reliving everything that had happened. It was easy enough to keep my body quiet, as the doctor had directed, but stilling the flow of emotion was impossible.

I prayed, of course, thanking God for His unfailing mercy and grace. I thanked Him for all of those who had had a part in my recovery and what I earnestly believed would be the restoration of my sight. I whistled hymns through my teeth and was relieved to feel no facial paralysis.

In the assurance of God's presence, I also slept. But during waking hours I played a game of "what if." What if:

. . . I hadn't gone for water before checking the storeroom?

. . . the fisherman had been on another part of the lake?

. . . the missionaries and their guest hadn't been visiting?

. . . the guest hadn't been a nurse?

. . . there had been no sample of a new antibiotic in her purse?

. . . the doctor had not appeared?

And so on and so on. This "what if" game went endlessly on.

And yet, I knew it wasn't a game at all. I knew that all of us at Lake Munkamba that morning had been participants with God in yet another of His unfathomable deeds. Had I been the object of an extraordinary series of coincidences? No, absolutely not. For in God's world, there are no coincidences.

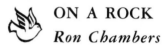

ON A ROCK
Ron Chambers

I was going snorkeling in the Palm Beach inlet with my fourteen-year-old son, Don, and our diving instructor, Jerry. We were to swim out past the jetty, then float into the channel with the tide. Yet I hesitated. The breakers were enormous.

I put on the foam rubber wet-vest and Jerry's weight belt to offset the vest's buoyancy. Actually, I knew that the weight should be adjusted for each diver, I just didn't think about that at the time.

We dove in, Jerry and Don paddling along in front, with me right behind. As we swam out, the distance between us grew. *Better swim harder,* I thought. But I was swimming as hard as I could. Halfway out I saw Jerry and Don clear the end of the jetty.

The next instant, a wave slammed me against the rocks. Then another and another. The barnacles on the boulders slashed my arms and legs. The heavy weight around my waist was dragging me down. I tried to grab on to the rocks, but they were too large, too slippery, too sheer.

Exhausted, battered, I knew right then that I was going to die. I was pleasantly surprised that I felt prepared for it. I imagined myself standing in the presence of God, and the thought gave me great peace. I looked up and said quietly, "I'm ready, Father . . ."

Needless to say, I did not die. I'm still mystified by the way I was saved. To this day I'm drawn often to Psalm 27:5: "For in the time of trouble, he shall hide me in his pavilion: . . . he shall set me up upon a rock."

In my time of trouble, a huge wave suddenly crashed into the jetty and a swirling column of water lifted me up, up, up, six feet in the air, spun me around in a sitting position, and placed me safely on top of a rock.

CALL ROY STANLEY
Christine Skillern

It was almost dark when I went into the kitchen to fix some supper. I didn't feel a bit hungry, but there are two rules we insulin-dependent diabetics must adhere to: take insulin regularly and don't skip meals.

So I shook some oatmeal into a pan of water, and set it to cooking on a front burner of my electric stove. I started across the kitchen to get milk from the refrigerator, but I never made it. My feet slipped out from under me and I fell hard, flat on my back, on the floor.

Oh, you've done it now, old girl.

I pushed and stretched and made every effort to get up, but I couldn't even sit up. Nothing I could do was going to get this overweight seventy-year-old body off the floor. I needed help. I thought about screaming, but who would hear me? I was a widow who lived alone and had already closed and locked all the windows and doors.

The telephone! I could call my sister, Martha. The telephone hung high on the wall, over near my bedroom door. Next to it was my broom, propped against the wall.

I dug my elbows into the rough texture of the floor covering and managed to slide on my back a couple of inches. Six or seven more shoves and a lot of panting put me near the phone. Using the broom, I gave it a *whack* that sent the handset banging to the floor. But to my dismay, I couldn't make a call. The dial was up on the phone.

Fear was beginning to gnaw at me. The burner under my oatmeal was glowing brightly. What would happen if the water boiled out? Would the metal pan melt and ruin my stove? Would it set my house on fire?

But there was nothing I could do. I was locked in my house with no way to contact the outside world, and no light except the glow from the electric burner.

Finally I whispered, "Lord Jesus, I'm so alone and I'm afraid. Please come and be here with me. Quiet me, Jesus, and protect me, and please take care of my pan of oatmeal."

The air began to chill as the evening grew longer. I hugged my arms about me and wished for a blanket. I dragged myself into the bedroom and looked longingly at the heavy spread on my bed. I could never pull that down. But there were some clothes lying on the cedar chest. Again I dug my elbows into the rug, and I pulled down a sweater and skirt to cover myself.

As the night grew blacker, I thought of the insulin shot I normally took after supper. What condition would I be in by morning? Was I going to die? My back was beginning to ache. I had no idea what damage I had done to myself. Panic began to smother me.

"Lord," I prayed, "don't leave me. Please stay with me and comfort me." Then I began to recite Scripture verses, mostly those I'd learned in Sunday school, one verse after another, until I slipped into a fitful sleep.

When the light of morning roused me, I thanked God that the long night was over and my house was not burned.

I said my morning prayers and made another attempt to get up from the floor. I could not move. My throat was dry and I was hungry. And how long could I go without insulin?

Surely a neighbor would telephone. Oh, no! The phone was off the hook. But then, maybe someone would come and knock on the door.

All morning I listened carefully but no knock came. I kept praying, "Jesus, please help me."

Around noon a thought flashed through my mind: *Call someone.*

Another thought: *Call your friends.*

"But the phone . . ." I said aloud.

I began to call out names. I started with my sister; I knew she'd be at work. Then I called my neighbors, one by one, pausing after each, listening for a knock.

I had run out of names to call when another sudden thought invaded my tired mind: *Call Roy Stanley.* Roy had stopped by two days earlier to pray with me, but he lived so far away.

Still the thought persisted: *Call Roy.*

So I began calling, "Roy, please come to me. I need you." I said it aloud, over and over without stopping.

It was about two o'clock when I heard a loud knocking on the back door. I yelled, "Come and help me. I need you."

Then I heard a series of heavy blows and a splintering of wood. Footsteps . . . and Roy was standing over me.

"Christine!" he exclaimed. "What are you doing on the floor?"

I told him.

Roy went to the kitchen to get some water for my parched throat. He phoned my sister and called for an ambulance. Then as we waited he told me how he happened to be there.

Roy and his wife were at home when he felt a strong urge to check on me. He told his wife, "I have to go to Christine. Something has happened to her."

When he knocked on my door, he got no answer, but something seemed to urge him, *Don't leave. Go to the back and knock again.* So he went around to the back door, knocked harder, and finally heard me calling, "Come and help me. I need you."

As the ambulance arrived, I felt a strange sense of elation. Jesus *had* been with me through the night. He'd brought Roy to rescue me. He'd answered every single one of my prayers. Even the one about the oatmeal. For when I finally thought about that burner, I said to Roy, "Will you please check on a pan of oatmeal I put on to cook last night? It must be burned black by now."

A strange expression crossed Roy's face. "I turned that burner off when I got the water for you," he said. "Did you say you put it on *last night?* Christine, that oatmeal is not burned. In fact, it's just ready to eat now!"

HE

Speaks

IN VISIONS

Of old thou didst speak in a vision . . .
—PSALM 89:19, RSV

SEEING BEYOND
—*Mildred N. Hoyer*

> See the blossom on the bare branch;
> See the harvest in the tiny seed;
> See the wholeness in the illness;
> See God's order in the confusion;
> See life in the midst of death—
> See the substance of things unseen.

THE SHARED DREAM
John Sherrill

In that mysterious Chapter 2 of the Book of Daniel, God saves
Daniel's life by revealing to him the content of King Nebuchad-
nezzar's dream. I'd long been awed by this story, for it spoke of
a dimension of the Spirit that was strange to me.

Then one stormy night my wife, Elizabeth, and I sat in front
of a fire with our friends Len LeSourd and his wife, Catherine
Marshall. After an hour of prayer we took a break. Catherine
made cocoa and our talk turned to the subject of dreams.

"I've had a recurring dream," said Catherine, leaning back in
her easy chair. "Every now and then I see myself in a—"

"Field," I said, interrupting. The room fell silent. Wind
blew a puff of smoke down the chimney.

"How did you know that?" Catherine asked softly.

What could I say? . . . Only that as she had begun to
describe her dream, I suddenly felt I knew its contents. I went
on, "You are standing in a flat field. There is a stream running
through the short, cropped grass . . ."

I knew from Catherine's expression that I was accurate. "The
peculiar thing about the scene," I concluded, "is that the creek
banks don't slant the way banks usually do. They're straight up
and down, yet they're not made by machinery."

And Catherine whispered that this was indeed the content of
her dream.

All of us were quiet for a while. I think each of us must have had the same thought. Here we were, people of the twentieth century, experiencing a mystery from the days of Daniel.

DREAM CHILD
Doris Lockerman

The woman's name was Mrs. Charles Smith. She was older than her years, and the long days of hard work on the farm had pulled at her face until there were no curves at all, only sweet, resigned lines. There was a peaceful look in her dark and strained eyes, the look of a woman who has not expected too much for a long time.

We were sitting in the farm house and she was telling me about her children.

She had borne three and lost all of them, she said, when they were babies. She never knew what it was that took them, maybe inadequate nourishment, perhaps the rigors of being born without a proper doctor. Whatever the cause, three of them had come here and been loved and then had died.

"Just as we felt they were doing pretty well."

Then one night, she said, she had a dream. She dreamed she would have another baby and she sobbed, "O Lord, don't send me another one, just to lose it!"

She said the voice in her dream told her not to fret, that this one would be a blessing . . .

Then Mrs. Smith looked across the bare room at a boy in his late teens, who sat looking out the window at some kittens and a puppy playing in the swept yard.

"You know, it was about that time that Ralph came to us." Her voice caressed him. "He can't hear," she said softly, "and he can't talk, but he's good. I don't know what we'd do without him."

Ralph turned then and smiled back at her, as if he had received a message. His eyes were blue and bright and intelligent. His work shirt was clean and stretched across strong, straight shoulders.

"He can read and write, and he works every day. He saves his money, and he bought us a little car. And we go to meetin' in it.

The boy flashed another smile and tried to speak. She whispered back at him, too low for ears to hear.

"He can read lips right well. My husband and I can talk to him without ever raising our voices. He understands us, and we understand him." She looked down, overcome by her own full heart.

"He came here from a cousin's home, when he was six, after his father died," she went on. "We raised him for our own. He was the child I dreamed about, the one who lived—he is the blessing."

THE DREAMED-ABOUT BABY
Katy Brown

The hot summer days of 1979 seemed to crawl by. My husband and I were waiting for our county adoption agency to complete the long process of clearing us so we could adopt a baby. We'd already gone through months of being interviewed and investigated—and we were told we would have another long wait even after we were approved.

Early one July morning, before dawn, I was startled awake by a vivid dream about a baby. What a happy dream *that* was—surely we'd have our baby soon!

But August passed without any developments, and September came before we even received our letter of clearance. Still, though our "credentials" were established, nothing happened. September dragged into October, and then November plodded by.

At last, two weeks before Christmas, the telephone call came. A woman at the adoption agency told me that the mother of a baby girl had reviewed the records of people and had chosen us. She gave me various details about the baby's birth and made an appointment for my husband and me to see her.

I hung up the phone and got out my desk calendar to mark

the date and time. Riffling through the pages, I saw a notation in my handwriting.

A prickle ran up my spine.

On the calendar page for July 20, I'd written "dreamed about baby."

That was the very day God had chosen for our adopted daughter to be born.

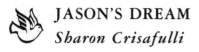

JASON'S DREAM
Sharon Crisafulli

"Good night, Jason." I leaned down and gently kissed my eight-year-old son's forehead as he snuggled under his comforter. He was wearing his favorite baseball pajamas. His hair, always a little too long, fanned out over the pillow. His eyes were already closed when I turned to leave. But as I was pulling the door shut, he called to me.

"Mom? I just had a dream."

I returned to Jason's bedside. "Honey, you haven't even been to sleep yet. How could you have had a dream?"

"I don't know, Mom. It just came to me right after I said my prayers." His brown eyes held a serious expression. "I was in school, at my desk," he said in a strange matter-of-fact tone. "All of a sudden, I fell over onto the floor. People were staring at me. I was dead."

I sat with Jason until he fell asleep. His "dream" was disturbing. It seemed more than just a child's imagination.

Several times in my life I'd had similar experiences. I remember suddenly knowing my grandmother would die. Though she appeared to be perfectly healthy, she left us three days later. And I remember being certain a seemingly happy couple were having deep marital difficulties. I don't know how I knew; I just knew. Outwardly, they were the picture of marital bliss. A year later they admitted they had been near divorce at the time.

I went to bed wondering what Jason's dream was all about. Was it some kind of warning?

By the following week, however, the incident had been pushed to the back of my mind. Our home in Merritt Island,

Florida, was a busy place, and I had plenty of other things to think about. Jason's school activities and caring for Nicole, his lively three-year-old sister, for example. Then one night a week later, I sat up abruptly in bed, wide awake. It was after midnight, and Jack, my husband, was sleeping soundly. For a moment I thought it was he who had woken me. But before I could give it another thought, I was overwhelmed with the need to pray—to pray for Jason.

As I eased out of bed, I felt tears streaming down my face. I crept into his room and gathered him into my arms. I cradled his warm body against mine as I prayed. I rocked him as I had when he was a baby. Jason slept soundly through it all.

Then it was over. The need to pray ended as suddenly as it had begun.

The next night it happened again—the sudden need to pray for Jason. And again the night after that.

There was a time in my life when I would have felt silly praying the way I did. There was a time when I would have told no one. There was a time when I would have been afraid.

But now I knew it was time to pray, and so I prayed.

By the third morning, my midnight prayers were becoming as predictable as the other routines of my life. As usual, I spent the few minutes before the children woke sipping coffee and savoring the quiet.

Nicole was usually the first to rise. But this morning she was still snoozing even after Jason was up and dressed for school.

It was gloomy and overcast. As I looked out the window, I was seized by a sense of sadness. Even as I made Jason's breakfast, my heart grew heavier by the moment.

I walked Jason to the end of our driveway. Right on time and with a whoosh of air brakes, the school bus pulled to a stop across the street, its red lights flashing.

Jason and I both looked up and down the busy highway. I gave him a quick kiss and he was on his way.

He never made it to the bus. His left foot had barely touched the pavement when a speeding station wagon came from nowhere and slammed into Jason, hurling his body fifteen feet into the air. He came down hard, headfirst.

It all happened so fast. Now, there he was, lying in the middle of the highway.

I fell to my knees beside him. His eyes were rolled back. His tongue was swollen and protruding. In a matter of seconds his right leg had swelled, straining the fabric of his jeans. His left arm was bent at a grotesque angle. I leaned close to his face and realized he wasn't breathing.

"No," I whispered. Then I lifted my head and screamed, "No, no, Lord, You can't let him die!"

A crowd gathered. They were all staring, horror-struck.

"Somebody call an ambulance!" I was amazed at the sudden control in my voice. "And get my husband. He's working in the orange grove down the road."

I bent over Jason and prayed aloud, "Dear God, I know You've raised people from the dead. Please raise up my son!"

I don't know how many people were in the crowd of onlookers, yet in their midst I suddenly felt a distinct presence. I glanced up and found myself looking straight into the eyes of a bearded man standing a few feet away. He had reddish-brown hair and stood relaxed with both hands in his pockets. Though it was only a second or two, it seemed like an eternity before he spoke in a surprisingly soft voice: "I have oxygen in my car."

Moments later the man knelt beside me and gently placed the mask over Jason's face. Almost instantly Jason gasped and drew a long breath. Weeping with relief, I leaned over and whispered into his ear, "It's okay, son, just think about Jesus. You're going to be okay."

But when I turned to thank the mysterious stranger, he was gone. And although the road was jammed in both directions, no one saw him leave.

Jason was in the hospital for months. His thigh and arm were broken. He had a severe concussion. But amazingly, there was no permanent damage.

Now, ten years later, I still shudder when I think about what might have happened if I had not heeded those urges to pray, and pray hard. You see, I know that the bearded man who saved Jason's life wasn't just some passing motorist. He was part of something bigger. Something that involved Jason's dream. Something that required my waking three nights in a row to pray for Jason.

That mysterious man was part of a heaven-directed rescue, and he was there in answer to my prayers.

A GIANT BESIDE OUR HOUSE
Ron Gullion

I'm in our yard on Big Fir Court, gazing up at the mighty two-hundred-fifty-foot tree the street is named for. Rising from the corner of our property to the height of a twenty-story building, the great white fir dwarfs our home and everything in sight like some ancient giant. It gives the illusion of leaning ominously toward me, creaking and swaying ever so slightly in the rustling wind.

Look! It's not leaning, it's falling! It's toppling toward our house, gaining momentum, rushing to meet its shadow, until finally it crumples the roof and splinters through the living room and front bedroom with a sickening, thunderous roar. I let out a cry. Alison's room!

I awoke in a drenching sweat and sat straight up trying to blink away the terrifying vision. Another nightmare. I slipped out of bed and stole a peek into Alison's room. Our nine-year-old daughter was sleeping peacefully, as was eleven-year-old Heath across the hall. But I couldn't shake the irrational fear until I'd checked. This was not the first time I'd dreamed of such an accident. In another dream I'd seen a giant tree limb tearing loose and slamming down on Heath, leaving him crippled.

As a computer engineer, I deal with quantifiable information. I don't pay much attention to impractical things like dreams. But these nightmares were so vivid and frightening. I eased back into bed next to my wife, Nita, but not before looking out the window at the tree. There it stood, stately and still, its coarse bark ghostly pale in the faint moonlight.

A few nights later I had another dream, this one more puzzling than alarming:

I am in our yard and in front of me stands a white angel. The angel has a broken wing.

What did all these dreams mean?

Then one day I noticed a twenty-foot dead limb dangling from the fir. Out here in the Northwest we call a dangerous limb like that a widow maker. I remembered the dream about Heath. "Don't go near that tree," I warned him. That Saturday I enlisted a neighbor to help me rope it down; all week I'd worried about the precarious branch. Later I had some other dead limbs removed too.

Why am I so concerned about this tree? I wondered. *It's stood here for generations. It even survived the fierce Columbus Day storm of '62.*

My nightmares about the tree eventually subsided. Christmas season arrived and Nita and I rushed madly to get our shopping done. More than anything, Alison wanted a Cabbage Patch doll. We scoured the stores around Portland with no luck. Everywhere we went it was the same story. "Sorry, folks," said the clerk inevitably. "We sold out our Cabbage Patch dolls weeks ago."

Finally Nita settled on a handmade rag doll. It was thicker and heavier than the Cabbage Patch version, but there was something about it that caught our fancy. "Well," sighed Nita as we paid for it, "this will have to do."

"Alison will love it," I reassured her.

We arrived home to a surprise. Alison had impetuously decided to rearrange her room. She'd been talking about it for days, but Nita had implored her to wait until the holiday excitement died down. "Then I'll help you," she'd promised.

Instead Alison had recruited her brother for the task, getting Heath to help drag her heavy bed across the room. "I just wanted to get it done now, Mommy," she explained as Nita surveyed the scene with obvious displeasure. "It's important." Alison's toys and furniture spilled out into the hall. By bed-time, however, Alison had her room in order again and we could scarcely hide our admiration.

"See?" said Alison knowingly. "It's not such a big deal."

Outside I heard the wind whistle through the big fir.

A howling blizzard marked Christmas Eve. I drove home from work through swirling snow and pounding winds. I pulled into the driveway, turned up my collar, and hurried inside to get ready for church. Church was not one of my priorities even under the best circumstances, and on a night like this I didn't want to be anywhere but inside my house, Christmas Eve or not. But I'd promised.

At the service with Nita and the kids, I felt strangely detached as I hunched in the pew with my arms folded tightly, thinking about whether I even believed that God was a part of my life. I'd been raised in church but that was a long time ago.

Now I certainly didn't feel any "tidings of comfort and joy." God may have created the world and all its wonders, but I didn't see where that had much to do with my life. If God was real, He was much too remote for me to have faith in.

We arrived home late, and the wind and snow stung our faces as we walked up the driveway. Heath and Alison rushed inside to turn on the Christmas tree lights. From our bay window the blue lights cast a peaceful glow across the snowy yard. I draped my arm around Nita and led her in.

Wrapping paper flew as the children tore into their presents, and Nita and I settled back on the couch to view the happy chaos. Nita had turned the tree into a work of art. The crowning touch was a glorious blond angel perched high at the top. "It looks like Alison," I said.

Alison was so delighted with her big new doll that she granted it the honor of accompanying her to bed. "Told you she'd love it," I reminded Nita as we climbed under the covers. The moaning wind lulled us to sleep.

Roar! The explosive sound jolted the house. I hadn't been asleep long, and my startled, half-awake mind tried to separate fantasy from reality. *The dream again,* I thought. But then I sat bolt upright, and suddenly I knew. This was no dream. This time my nightmare was real. The tree really had fallen on our house!

I leapt out of bed and raced across the hall to Alison's room. "Daddy, help!" she was calling frantically. "I'm stuck!"

I couldn't budge the door. It was jammed shut. "Oh, my God," I whispered. "Don't move, honey!" I shouted through the door. "We'll get you out." I grabbed a flashlight and told Nita to call 911. "I'll see if I can get to her from outside."

I was horrified to find the tree filling the front hall, branches whipping in the gale. I stumbled through the family room to a side door. Outside I nearly collided with the massive trunk. Propped up on its giant ball of roots, which had been torn from the earth, it looked prehistoric. I crawled underneath as the rough bark tore at my robe and ripped my flesh. The wind sliced through me. Above the din I heard the distant wail of sirens.

Groping my way to Alison's window I aimed the flashlight beam inside and wiped the icy snow from my eyes. All I could see were branches, tattered insulation, and hunks of ceiling strewn about the trunk. Somewhere buried beneath the tree was my daughter, crying faintly, "Daddy! Daddy!"

Someone was standing beside me. "Alison! This is Captain McCullough of the fire department," he called. "Your daddy's with me. Can you move at all?"

"I think I can move my arm," came a brave little voice.

"Good. Push you hand up as high as you can."

Tiny fingers wriggled up through the debris. I breathed a tentative sigh of relief. Firemen rushed to set up lights and heat lamps. They fastened a plastic tarp over the rescue area. Captain McCullough turned to me and said quietly, "This isn't going to be easy, Mr. Gullion."

As I huddled with Nita, and neighbors looked after Heath, a terrifying game of pick-up sticks slowly unfolded. The night air was filled with the roar of chain saws and the reek of fir pitch as rescuers cut away at the tree and cautiously removed branches as they went. A slight shift of any debris could spell disaster.

Bit by bit they chipped away at the wreckage until, after an hour, Alison's head and shoulders emerged. Her right leg appeared to be crushed under the tree. A fallen two-by-six rafter clamped down on her torso. We could see Alison's new doll squeezed between her chest and the rafter. Apparently she'd fallen asleep clutching it.

McCullough shook his head grimly and called a halt to the work. "We can't risk it," he said. "Show me the crawl space." Moments later he played his flashlight on the area under Alison's room. Limbs a half foot in diameter pierced the floor and stabbed the ground beneath. Again McCullough shook his head. "We can't cut away the floor without disturbing the tree. *And that tree must not shift.*"

The subzero wind had intensified. Hours had passed and now there was the threat of Alison succumbing to hypothermia. Neighbors rushed in warm blankets and hot-water bottles. A paramedic put his wool ski cap on Alison's head. But I could see she was drifting, her big eyes fluttering. Once or twice her head rolled back. If we didn't get her leg out soon, the surgeons might have to amputate it to free her.

Only one chance was left: to lift the tree. A crane was out of the question. In this wind it would be too unstable. But

McCullough had called a towing company that used giant air bags to gently right overturned semitrailers. "It's a gamble," he warned me. "But we've run out of options."

Huge rubber bags were packed under the tree. A compressor roared to life. Slowly the bags filled with air and swelled against the giant fir. Despite the blizzard, I could see sweat bead up on McCullough's tensed brow. My hands trembled as Nita buried her head in my chest, afraid to look.

Suddenly I heard myself praying to the God whose very existence, just hours earlier, I'd doubted. You would have thought I'd be ashamed to ask His help now, but something told me I must. "Please, Lord," I begged, "spare her life. I believe You are there."

The shriek of the compressor was deafening. The bags bulged like great billows, but at first nothing gave.

Then there was movement! Inch by agonizing inch, the tree was lifted. A cry rose from the crowd as paramedics rushed to free Alison and whisk her to a waiting ambulance. Nita and I jumped in with her, and we roared off. Alison smiled weakly. "I'll be okay now, Daddy," she whispered, still grasping her new doll.

That overstuffed doll, it turned out, was possibly just enough of a cushion between the fallen two-by-six rafter and Alison's chest to have saved her life.

The doctors confirmed that she would recover. And Alison's leg was only broken, not crushed.

Christmas Day, Heath and I kicked through the rubble of our house. I'd been thinking about that desperate prayer I'd said, thinking about it a lot. In Alison's room I saw that the bulk of the fir had landed near the southeast wall—right where her bed had been before she'd impulsively moved it. On the trunk directly over where Alison lay when the tree came crashing through, I noticed a wide scar from a recently cut branch—one of those I'd felt such urgency to remove after my dream. That branch might have killed her.

Had God been trying to warn me all along about the tree? To protect us? Had I been blind to God's ways?

In the snow outside what used to be our living room I found the angel from our Christmas tree, the one that looked like Alison. Its wing was broken, just as the angel's wing in my dream had been. As I brushed it off and held it up, Heath came running. "Dad, Dad!" He grabbed the angel. "I've seen this before! In a dream! An angel with a broken wing just like this one!"

Dreams. Does God speak to us through them? The Bible says He does (Job 33:14–18), as well as in many other ways. This much I myself can say: Alison is safe and well. And God is, and always has been, watching over my family.

AFTER THE STORM
—Hilen Letiro

> The storms may come
> And limbs may break;
> Yet others bend
> Beneath the weight—
> Of heavy rain
> And windy breeze. . .
> A storm can mark
> The strongest trees.
>
> Life sometimes deals
> With us this way;
> In unseen trials
> We meet each day.
> It's not how much our bodies break
> Or how much they may bend;
> It's our outlook in our own life
> That helps our spirits mend.

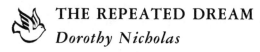

THE REPEATED DREAM
Dorothy Nicholas

I've always been impressed by the way men and women in the

Bible were guided by dreams—from the angels climbing Jacob's ladder to the dream warning Joseph to flee with his family to Egypt. I've always known such things were possible, but it was only in 1978 that I received such a dream myself.

A dear friend had a terminal illness and yearned to see her son again. The young man led a nomadic life. He didn't keep in touch very closely, and when he telephoned he rarely told her where he was.

Then one night I had a strange dream of huge stacks of *Esquire* magazines. I couldn't recall ever having read the magazine. I dismissed the dream as being of no significance, but it persisted. After I dreamed of a house built entirely out of *Esquire* magazines, my husband bought a copy. But I saw nothing helpful in it.

Then one day, a sudden thought hit me—the name of a hotel in Chicago that somehow I connected with the son. Did he live there? When I was visiting my friend, I contrived to sneak a peek at her address book. There, next to her son's name, among years of addresses, I saw the name of the hotel.

I wrote a letter to the son at that address, telling him of his mother's illness.

That was Monday. At eleven o'clock on Thursday night, my friend's son called collect from Chicago. He'd only been back at the hotel for a few days and he'd just received my letter. Shortly before his mother's death, he was reunited with her.

Dreams can be very real, and anytime I'm tempted to just brush one off, I remember the name of that hotel.

The Esquire, just like the magazine.

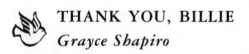

THANK YOU, BILLIE
Grayce Shapiro

How much of a married couple's time together is spent in quiet pleasures, such as eating breakfast in the morning sun or enjoying an evening walk! Even late at night, when my husband was asleep, I enjoyed reading and writing and thinking, knowing he was there.

But when Billie died, those simple pleasures died with him. I was too tense to sleep. Each moment that I was awake and each tick of the clock reminded me that he wasn't there. I'd fall asleep only as dawn was breaking, and be wakened moments later by my alarm.

On one such morning I drowsily stumbled into the kitchen, put on the tea kettle, then wandered back into the bedroom and lay down on the bed. Instantly I was fast asleep, the deep exhausted sleep that finally comes, but never when I wanted it to. I had a dream. Billie and I were in the kitchen preparing coffee and toast. I saw him taking bread out of the bag and putting it in the toaster. I could hear him asking me if the water was boiling yet. Suddenly he became stern, saying, "Darling, you have the kettle on the wrong burner." And he repeated himself. Then he yelled, *"Darling, you have it on the wrong burner!"*

I jumped to my feet. There was an overpowering smell of gas in the room. The stove! The pilot light that I hadn't repaired! I dashed to the kitchen, turned off the stove, threw open the windows.

"Oh, thank You, God!" I cried out. And then I added the words that changed my life, "Thank you, Billie."

 ## THE CROWN OF THORNS
Caryll Houselander

As a child during World War I, I attended a French convent school. One of the nuns was from Bavaria. She spoke little English and very poor French, and she made no real contact with the children. Local police interrogated her as an "enemy alien," and there were even subtle murmurs in the community that she was a spy dressed as a nun. As the Germans advanced, so did the nun's loneliness and isolation.

One day as I passed the bootroom, the little cubicle where our shoes were kept, I saw the Bavarian nun sitting alone, cleaning shoes. I can see her now as if it were yesterday—a tall, gaunt woman with brilliant red cheeks, and eyes so dark that they looked black. There she was, wearing her large, cobalt-blue apron, with a child's pair of shoes on her lap.

Then I noticed the tears running down her rosy cheeks and falling onto the shoes. Abashed, I dropped my eyes to her large toil-worn hands. Hands, red and chapped, with blunted nails, which were folded in a way that expressed inconsolable grief.

We were both quite silent, I staring away not wanting to see her crying.

At last, when I raised my head, I saw an unbelievable sight: the nun's head was circled by a crown of thorns.

I shall not attempt to explain this. I am simply telling the thing as I saw it. That bowed head was weighed down under the crown.

I stood dumbfounded a few seconds, and then I told her, "I would not cry if I were wearing the crown of thorns like you are."

She looked startled, and asked, "What do you mean?"

I sat down beside her, and as I described to her what I had seen, a glow of joy enveloped her, dispelling the grief.

Together we polished the children's shoes.

 ## AT THE FOOT OF THE CROSS
Ernest Borgnine

Back in 1975 I was offered a part in the film *Jesus of Nazareth,* which through the years has been shown at Easter time on NBC television. Our cast, directed by the renowned Franco Zeffirelli, included Anne Bancroft as Mary Magdalene and Olivia Hussey as Mary, mother of Jesus. I played the part of the centurion who was present at the crucifixion, the one whose servant had been healed by Jesus.

Much of the film was shot in Tunisia on the Mediterranean during January and February of 1976. A cold, damp wind continually knocked over floodlights and stung us with desert sand. I was uncomfortable in my thick leather uniform. My neck ached under a ponderous metal helmet, and I even began to pity those ancient Roman soldiers who were called centurions because they commanded a hundred men.

When it came time for my scene during the crucifixion, the weather was chill and gray. The camera was to be focused on me at the foot of the cross, and so it was not necessary for Robert Powell, the actor who portrayed Jesus, to be there. Instead, Zeffirelli put a chalk mark on a piece of scenery beside the cameraman. "I want you to look up at that mark," he told me, "as if you were looking at Jesus."

"Okay," I said, moving into position and looking up at the mark as instructed.

"Ready?"

I hesitated. Somehow I wasn't ready. I was uneasy.

"Do you think it would be possible for somebody to read from the Bible the words Jesus said as He hung on the cross?" I asked.

I knew the words well from the days of my childhood in an Italian-American family in Connecticut, and I'd read them in preparation for the film. Even so, I wanted to hear them now.

"I will do it myself," Zeffirelli said. He found a Bible, opened it to the Book of Luke, and signaled for the camera to start rolling.

As Zeffirelli began reading Christ's words aloud, I stared up at that chalk mark, thinking what might have gone through the centurion's mind.

That poor Man up there, I thought. *I met Him when He healed my servant, who is like a son to me. Jesus says He is the Son of God, an unfortunate claim during these perilous times. But I know He is innocent of any crime.*

"Father, forgive them; for they know not what they do." The voice was Zeffirelli's, but the words burned into me—the words of Jesus (Luke 23:34–46).

Forgive me, Father, for even being here, was the centurion's prayer that formed in my thoughts. *I am so ashamed, so ashamed.*

"Verily I say unto thee, today shalt thou be with me in paradise," said Jesus to the thief hanging next to Him.

If Jesus can forgive that criminal, then He will forgive me, I thought. *I will lay down my sword and retire to my little farm outside of Rome.*

Then it happened.

As I stared upward, instead of the chalk mark, I suddenly saw the face of Jesus Christ, lifelike and clear. It was not the features of Robert Powell I was used to seeing, but the most beautiful, gentle visage I have ever known. Pain-seared, sweat-stained, with blood flowing down from thorns pressed deep, His face was still filled with compassion. He looked down at me through tragic, sorrowful eyes with an expression of love beyond description.

Then His cry rose against the desert wind. Not the voice of Zeffirelli, reading from the Bible, but the voice of Jesus Himself: "Father, into thy hands I commend my spirit."

In awe I watched Jesus' head slump to one side. I knew He was dead. A terrible grief welled within me, and completely oblivious of the camera, I started sobbing uncontrollably.

"Cut!" yelled Zeffirelli. Olivia Hussey and Anne Bancroft were crying too. I wiped my eyes and looked up again to where I had seen Jesus—He was gone.

Whether I saw a vision of Jesus that windswept day or whether it was only something in my mind, I do not know. It doesn't matter. For I do know that it was a profound spiritual experience and that I have not been quite the same person since. I believe that I take my faith more seriously. I like to think that I'm more forgiving than I used to be. As that centurion learned two thousand years ago, I too have found that you simply cannot come close to Jesus without being changed.

 ## HE IS A PATH
—Giles Fletcher

> He is a path, if any be misled;
> He is a robe, if any naked be;
> If any chance to hunger, He is bread;
> If any be a bondman, He is free;
> If any be but weak, how strong is He!
> To dead men, life is He; to sick men, health;
> To blind men, sight; and to the needy, wealth . . .

HE Sends

HIS WORD

So they cried to the Lord in their trouble,
and he saved them from their distress;
he sent his word to heal them
and bring them alive out of the pit of death.
Let them thank the Lord for his enduring love
and for the marvellous things he has done.

—PSALM 107:19–21, NEB

ST. PATRICK'S ARMOR
—From St. Patrick's breastplate

I bind unto myself today
The power of God to hold and lead,
His eye to watch, His might to stay,
His ear to hearken to my need,
The wisdom of my God to teach,
His hand to guide, His shield to ward;
The word of God to give me speech,
His heavenly host to be my guard.

THROUGH THE FIRE
Nellia B. Garber

The Bible was a gift from Bob, my husband, but it seemed to belong as much to our son, Doug, as it did to me. Doug and I read it together. We shared it in Bible study groups. Together we underlined God's promises. So when I received a new Bible, this familiar one became Doug's own.

Doug married, and eventually he and his family moved into a house not far from ours. Driving an eighteen-wheeler, he spent long hours away from home. He kept a little leather pocket Bible with him in the rig, but he made sure that "our" Bible stayed safely at home.

Then one bitter winter afternoon, there was a fire. He and Marla and the three boys were in despair. "The whole house burned down," Doug told us. "We lost everything."

For a week, neighbors, family, and friends tried to help them. They supplied clothes, money, food, furniture, and many prayers. Then one day Marla came over, smiling.

"Mom," she said, "look what I found in the rubble." Into my hands she laid an old Bible, soaking wet, its leather cover shriveled and brittle, but with all the pages intact. Doug's Bible—*our* Bible.

Immediately I began to dry it, first with a towel, then in the oven at 150 degrees. Slowly it became supple enough for me to turn its pages. When Doug came home, I said excitedly, "Open it up. Just let it fall open."

The Good Book opened and Doug read a passage we had underlined: *When thou passest through the waters, I will be with thee . . . when thou walkest through the fire, thou shalt not be burned; neither shall the flame kindle upon thee* (Isaiah 43:2).

God's promises. God's precious promises.

 ## THE HIDDEN HAND OF GOD . . .
Clared Holmes

One night a few years ago, for no apparent reason, I awakened in the middle of the night with a deep sense of foreboding. I checked the children but they were sleeping peacefully.

Before retiring I had, as usual, prayed for God's protection for the family and especially for my husband, Jim, who drove a cab on the night shift. Was God now trying to tell me something?

Once more I made the rounds of the house, sniffing the air for traces of leaking gas or the odor of burning; all was well.

I returned to my bedroom. The thought became clearer that Jim was in acute danger. I was overwhelmed with fear.

"God, please tell me what is Thy will. What am I to do?" I prayed, the sense of urgency keen. Opening my Bible at random, the words seemed to stand out: "Be still, and know that I am God" (Psalm 46:10).

Be still. Silence, fear. *Know that I am God.* Know without a doubt that God has His everlasting wings around every one of His children, guarding and protecting them.

Jim and I had always been very close spiritually, so now I spoke aloud to him across the miles:

"Jim, be still. *Be still.* Right where the danger is, there God is, protecting you. But you must *be still* and listen."

I glanced at the clock. It was 2:07 A.M. I felt God's presence very close and I knew all was well.

The next morning when Jim returned home, he related a

curious happening. He had been about to descend one of San Francisco's steepest hills with two passengers when he heard a voice say, "Be still." He lifted a foot from the throttle, half turned in his seat, and asked, "Did you speak?" The passengers claimed they had not spoken. He turned, was about to proceed, when he heard again, "Be still."

He was rolling slowly, but now the thought came to him: *Test your brakes.* Just as the front wheels went over the crest of the hill, he put his foot on the brake and discovered they were quite useless. He made an abrupt turn and rammed the cab against a cement retaining wall. The front of the cab was mangled, but no one was injured.

"If I'd gone two feet farther," Jim said, "we could have had a terrible disaster. I couldn't have stopped the car and we might have hit other autos at the intersection.

"It must have been God speaking to me, telling me to be still so I could hear the thought to test my brakes."

"What time was this?" I asked.

"I picked up the passengers a few minutes after two," he replied.

 ## FAREWELL ON THE MOUNTAINSIDE
Betty Banner

Snow had fallen all night and the mountain was a fairyland of whiteness. I was twenty-one years old and expecting my first baby in the spring. All my life until the past ten months had been spent in a fairly good-sized town, and the deep, narrow valley between the tall mountain and ridge where I was living with my husband and his mother was a constant source of interest and new experiences. The mountain folks I had come to know and the many customs of the "old folks" that they still cherished had formed a new world for me.

During the previous summer I had insisted that we attend the little white Methodist church about two miles down the valley, and even though the circuit-rider preacher only came

once a month, I had helped organize a Sunday school for the in-
between time.

This particular morning was Monday and "washday" by an
infallible rule of the mountain community. Snow or no snow,
we washed, and I hummed a gay little tune as I helped my
mother-in-law fill the zinc tubs on the glowing kitchen range
and sorted the clothes for washing. My thoughts were of the
coming baby, and the warm, steamy kitchen, accentuated by
the white coldness seen through the windows, gave me a feeling
of security and snugness. In thinking of my own happiness, I
talked with my mother-in-law about the pity we felt for a young
couple, who, we had been told, had lost their three-week-old
baby during the night just the day before. We were still
speculating as to what might have caused such a death when a
knock at the back door gave us both a start.

Opening the door we were even more startled to see standing
there the very same father of the dead child we had just been
discussing. His name was John and he seemed hesitant to come
into the kitchen but stood twirling his cap in his hands and
staring at his feet. All of a sudden he took a deep breath and
blurted out, "Betty, we was aimin' to bury our baby today, and
now this snow an' all, and the preacher can't get acrost the
ridge, and from the way hit's snowin' can't reckon when he
could get here." Then as we started to sympathize, he said, "My
Maude . . . she's right smart tore up, and ain't able to git outta
bed this mornin', but she says we just can't put our baby away
'lessen we have a service over her, and you're the only one I
knowed round here I thought could do it."

It was a moment before my stunned brain could take it in
that he was talking to and about me. I couldn't believe he was
asking me to do the service. I started to stammer that I couldn't
possibly preach a funeral, and besides we couldn't get the car
out of the shed even to go two miles down the valley. I might
have saved my breath, for he stood there with such grief and
stubborn determination in his eyes that I felt like I was butting
my head against a brick wall for all the progress I was making.

Then he said quietly, "How'd you feel if it was your young
'un?" That did it. I had no answer for that, so I dumbly wiped
my still wet hands on my apron and began to untie it. I don't
remember another word spoken as I pulled on high rubber boots

and coat and muffler. All I could do was pray frantically over and over, "Dear God, help me, give me words to help. Help me to say what will comfort them, Lord. . . . "

Leaving word about where I was going for my husband who was feeding cattle, I set out with John for the long cold walk to the church. Slipping, sliding, often wading drifts, with no conversation between us, the silent white flakes of snow pounding in our faces, we reached the church at last and went in. My heart came up into my throat. In spite of the snow, the little chapel was filled with mountain folks, and the little homemade coffin rested under a wreath of crepe-paper flowers in front of the rough altar.

Such a small, crude little chapel, with its oil lamps hanging on the walls, yet in that moment it seemed to me as vast and awesome as St. Patrick's Cathedral, which I once visited. I thought I'd never reach the front and as I stumbled down the aisle, my frantic brain could only repeat the same prayer: "Dear God, help me, help me. Let me say the words that will help them feel Your presence."

When I turned to face the silent congregation, I had to grip the pine pulpit tightly to keep from just going down. It hit me, too, that there was not even a Bible in front of me and I had not thought to bring mine!

As I realized that, I thought, *Well, this is it. I cannot go any further.* And then my eyes fell on that pitiful little box. Then and there God worked a miracle for me, just as surely as if He had reached out and touched my mind and lips. From somewhere unknown, the words came, disjointed as to correctness of quotation I am sure, but essentially those I had heard from early childhood on similar occasions. "I am the resurrection and the life . . ." "Casting all your care upon him for he careth for you." "Suffer the children to come unto me . . . for of such is the kingdom of heaven." On and on the words came, as if a scroll were being unwound before my eyes. Last of all came a prayer—and that was mine, for as I felt my own unborn child stir within me, my petition for a grieving mother in a log cabin on that lonely mountainside found the right words for the final commitment of "earth to earth" at the tiny graveside.

I am now a grandmother, and through the years I have faced many trials and crosses where I have felt like giving up before I started. But always the memory of "my miracle" comes to me and I go on, for surely the loving God who could give an ignorant twenty-one-year-old girl a funeral service can guide a more mature woman through any difficulty. Always, too, in such a crisis I seem to see John's face and hear the simple words he spoke as I turned from that grave toward home.

"Thank you—I knowed you could do it."

SHOW ME YOU LOVE ME, LORD
Janet Martin

Do you believe in miracles? I do, because one happened to me. Let me tell you about it.

In those days, I was a virtual newlywed, having been married two years to a young dentist. Wyman and I were living in Altus, Oklahoma, then; he was serving a tour with Uncle Sam at the Air Force base in that Panhandle town.

The wind blows constantly in Altus, moaning down chimneys, whirling dust into blood-red sunsets, and piling mounds of loose, scraggly tumbleweed against front doors. It can be a lonely sound, wind, particularly when it heralds the approach of midwestern winter.

I was not lonely that first November away from my Georgia home, however. Busy with my first house, looking forward to a first Christmas in a new town, I was anticipating another first— the coming of a child into our lives.

Due in January, he (I simply knew it was a boy) would fill up the extra bedroom with diapers and stuffed animals, smells of talcum powder and sounds of contentment. His crib had been ordered; his room newly painted. It was about two weeks before Thanksgiving, and I looked like I had swallowed the turkey.

"It's going to be a football player," my husband laughed as I waddled, seven months pregnant, from stove to table, fixing dinner the night of November 7, 1971.

"Wait a minute!" I shot back. "I still look pretty good from the neck up. Focus on that!"

The night was cold. After dinner we lit a fire, watched the dancing flames, talked of quiet hopes, and called it a day.

Then, without warning, in the middle of the night, a gush of water, and I awoke, knowing something was terribly wrong. I called the doctor.

"Your water has probably broken," he said. "You might go into labor or the sac might seal off. Call me if it doesn't, but in the meantime, lie down. Keep me informed."

Later, I learned, Dr. Richard Hagood had turned from the receiver to his wife, Dana, a friend of mine. "Janet's carrying twins," he said worriedly.

Meanwhile, I hung up the telephone, strangely calm. I told Wyman what the doctor had said, then lay down on the bed and went to sleep.

The dawn of November 8 seeped around the window shade, which rattled loosely in the wind. I sensed its coming and knew I would be going to the hospital that day.

In the emergency room I smiled at my doctor friend as he strode in carrying X rays that had been taken moments before. "Janet," he said, "I've got something to show you."

Slap, slap went the X-ray film, gray against the fluorescent view box on the wall. There, glowing from the screen, were two tiny shapes, twins, impatient to be born two months early.

Because the hospital in Altus was small, Dr. Hagood thought it urgent that I be in a larger hospital facility, one especially equipped to handle "preemies." Wilford Hall Hospital, the medical center at Lackland Air Force Base, San Antonio, Texas, was such a place. That was where I should go, the doctors decided, and somehow they arranged for a plane to fly me there. My husband, close by my side, was pale, anxious. He knew the survival odds on premature infants. I did not.

At Wilford Hall, everyone in the labor room was kind, but businesslike. A nurse came in, heavy, motherly. "These are your first," she stated, rather than asking. I nodded. "I hope they're girls," she smiled. Then she said something I thought was strange: "Girls do better."

But they were boys. Blond, blue-eyed, curly haired, and beautiful. They lived only twenty-four hours.

Back in Oklahoma, numb with shock, I greeted my concerned friends with a blank face. I looked at my husband's face, lined with grief, and felt remote from everything. The doorbell rang. A delivery boy had brought the baby crib. Would I sign for it?

Wyman and I boxed up the tiny pink and blue clothes we had purchased for a layette. My mother, who had flown out to be with us, suggested that we close the nursery door for a while. We did. And I closed the door to my heart.

Time moved on. Holidays—Thanksgiving, Christmas—came and went. I hardly noticed. Somehow Wyman and I finished our Air Force tour, aided by the comfort and support of good friends. Our departure date was set. We were going back to Georgia. We were leaving the lonely prairie wind that had blown my grief-stricken thoughts around and around until I thought I would go mad.

Would my heart ever heal? Would the sadness ever soften? Would the questions ever cease?

The morning we were to set off for Georgia, I sat down amid the packed cardboard boxes and opened my Bible. Pressing two thumbs together at random on the gilt-edged pages, I spread the book out across my knees. Incredulously, I read words I had never seen before: "Sing, O barren one, who did not bear; break forth into singing and cry aloud. . . . For the children of the desolate one will be more. . . ."

Isaiah, the prophet, continued to speak, especially to me, it seemed, in this marvelous fifty-fourth chapter! "Enlarge the place of your tent, and let the curtains of your habitations be stretched out; hold not back. . . ." For a moment, reading those ancient words, I felt a flicker of hope.

But the house in Georgia seemed big, too big for a young couple with no children. While my husband was at work, I walked the hollow halls. I closed barren bedroom doors. I listened for voices that would never frolic here, and I came face-to-face with despair.

Enlarge the place of your tent. But this tent only housed the wind.

I kept trying, however. I sewed curtains, cleaned carpets. I bought a cat and lavished attention on her as if she were human. Wyman and I thought up things to do, places to go, friends to see. But something was missing. We both knew it. And we could not seem to do anything about it.

A year passed, a long terrible year. Another was well on its way, and despite our longings, our prayers, there was no baby on our horizon.

I went to work to forget. A journalism job—new challenges, the exciting smell of newspapers coming black and smudgy off giant rollers—these things helped. But busyness was only a temporary relief.

Finally in desperation I went to the Source. I opened the door of my heart to God. Alone one morning early in February, I stretched out my arms flat across the kitchen table, bent my head, and cried. I told the Author of life I could not bear the hurt and emptiness any more. I wanted to die.

"Lord," I sobbed brokenly, "if I must go on living, You have got to show me You love me. I can't help it, Lord. Maybe it's not right to ask for a sign, but I feel so alone, I feel You don't love me, Lord. Please, if it's not too much to ask, show me You do."

Slowly, quietly, spring came to Georgia. Swollen dogwood buds burst into tiny white crosses. Crocuses peered through the sodden red clay. The pine tree pollen blew in the gentle Southern breezes, sprinkling all nature with a powdery yellow glaze.

And as life stirred all around us, my prayer was heard. We were expecting a baby again.

Enlarge the place of your tent. Hold not back . . .

We bought a tiny yellow cotton nightgown. Months moved by, and we hung curtains in one of the empty bedrooms. Then, almost trembling, we unpacked the unused baby crib; we unboxed tiny pink and blue clothes.

When the seventh month of pregnancy came, I was afraid. I had terrible dreams. But the seventh month passed, and the eighth.

Then, early in the ninth month, it happened again. I was lying quietly on the bed that afternoon, reading a book. Suddenly, my water broke.

Frantically, I called the doctor. "Don't you see?" I screamed at him. "It is November eighth! The twins were born this way exactly two years ago today!"

"I understand that, Janet," Dr. Robert Davis replied calmly. "But I believe the Lord works in mysterious ways. I'll meet you at the hospital. Get going."

Show me You love me, Lord . . .

Our daughter was born safe and whole, within minutes of the time when the twins had come. Early the next morning, when the nurses rolled that tiny pink bundle into my room, I cried for joy. I took little Kristen in my arms, kissed her beet-red nose, and said "Thank You" to the God who had showed me that He loved me.

There are some, I know, who would look upon all this as coincidence. There might even be statistical wizards who could calculate the probability of a same birth date—even the same birth hour—within the realm of reasonable expectation. But their opinions would be irrelevant to me.

All I knew then, and what I still know, is that death was swallowed up in life.

And because of that, because the Lord took personal care to express His love to me in that special way, I believe in miracles. And today when I read the fifty-fourth chapter of Isaiah, I know why He issued such a strange command to that newly barren young woman in Oklahoma years ago. He was telling me that in the face of trouble I should have faith. I should sing.

A CIRCLE OF LITTLE RED CHAIRS
Philip Turner

The May night was balmy, with no hint of disaster in the moonlit sky, when our neighbor, a pilot, said, "Let's take a midnight spin over the lake." Just as casually as that. My wife, Bobbie, and I told Bob we'd love to go. Just as casually as that, on Memorial Day weekend in 1975, our lives were changed . . .

At Shelbyville's small airport, deserted at that hour, I watched Bobbie climb into the little four-seater Beech Musketeer first, her tall athletic figure folding into the space behind the tiny cockpit. I took the copilot's seat while Bob ran the safety checks. This was a good little adventure for us. Bobbie and I hadn't been spending much time together in the last year or so. My law practice kept me running six days a week. As for Bobbie, with the kids both in school, she needed more to do than play golf, so she'd begun to travel all over Illinois as an instructor for Weight Watchers. We communicated with notes on the kitchen table. Bobbie and I were drifting apart, and both of us knew it.

In a few minutes we'd left the runway lights behind and were climbing into that crystal clear sky. Below us in the moonlight Shelbyville was asleep. I could see my parents' house where the children were sleeping over. The law office I shared with my father. The church where Bobbie and the kids went. They went, but I didn't. Sunday was the day I caught up on my sleep.

I wasn't an atheist, I'd explained to the kids. As a lawyer I acknowledged a Divine Law. But I didn't expect that Law to take time out from running the universe to look after me. My own hard work did that. I'd already become state's attorney for Shelby County, and—

"Look there!" Bob said.

The cloud dropped out of nowhere, a "low scud" suddenly obscuring the moon. Bob nosed the plane downward to stay beneath it.

"Better go back," he decided. No telling how far the fog extended.

Bob began a slow 180-degree turn, descending all the while to keep below that rapidly falling ceiling. I could see the runway lights ahead of us now, off to the left.

It's the last thing I remember. The rest of what happened I pieced together weeks later from other people.

They say it was the nose wheel of the Musketeer that hit the power line, flipping the plane over. In the split second before it hit the ground upside down, Bob's reflexes were quick enough to switch off the electrical system, preventing us all from being cremated on the spot.

Bobbie was somehow thrown over my head and through the side window onto the ground.

I am told that I remained suspended head downward in my seat belt, with over a hundred bone fractures.

Trapped inside the smashed cockpit and badly injured himself, Bob could only wonder why rescue was so long in coming. From the tail of the plane, he knew, an automatic crash-signal would be broadcasting our whereabouts.

What Bob did not know was that the only electronically equipped facility in range, the Federal Aviation Agency's flight service station in Decatur, twenty-five miles away, never received the signal. Our plane was upside down, the transmitter stuck in the ground. In the normal course of events it would be next morning at the soonest, long after the three of us were dead, before anyone happened out in this direction and spotted the wreckage of the Musketeer.

A few miles away, however, a woman who happened to be a client of mine was watching a late TV show when all the lights in her house went out. She called the electric company, who roused a sleepy repairman. He found the line into the woman's house intact and, climbing back into his truck, set out to look for the break.

An hour and a half after the accident he spotted the downed plane and radioed the sheriff. As chief law enforcement officer for the county I had worked with the sheriff for several years; my face was so swollen he never recognized me. I don't remember the trip by ambulance to the local hospital, where our injuries were treated. Nor being transferred together with Bobbie and Bob to the larger hospital in Decatur.

I first regained consciousness in the intensive-care unit. Dimly I became aware of the small curtained cubicle, the whir of machinery. I seemed to recall being in an airplane, and that Bobbie had been with me, but the scattered images refused to come together.

What filled my mind was something else. Something glowing, alive—and impossibly huge. A presence unimaginably vast was somehow with me in that tiny space. More than with me. It was containing me, enfolding me, cradling me. I was being *held* as a baby is held. A baby who has only just opened its eyes to behold the Father who has carried it all along.

Hours passed. Doctors bent over, tubes were removed and inserted, and all the while I was wrapped in that bright cocoon I could only call Love.

As my head grew clearer, and still that love embraced me, I began to argue with it. I was accustomed, after all, to argue cases on their merit. Why should God love me? God was the only name I could give to the glory that radiated in that six-by-three cubicle. But I hadn't given God much of a thought in thirty years.

Not that we loved God, 1 John 4:10 corrected me, *but that he loved us.* . . .

Who hath saved us, I recalled too, from 2 Timothy 1:9, *not according to our works, but according to his own purpose and grace.*

I blinked my eyes. Where were these verses coming from? I hadn't opened a Bible in years, and I certainly had never memorized—

And then I remembered Sunday school (I must have been five years old), a little circle of small red chairs, a cluster of children, and old Mrs. Wolf with a Bible open on her lap. She drilled us on Bible verses. Those who could recite the memory verses got a pretty card to keep. I didn't collect many cards; I was one of Mrs. Wolf's disappointments.

The painful days in the ICU dragged on. Strange, above the rattle of instrument carts, I heard Mrs. Wolf's voice:

Fear not. . . .

God so loved the world. . . .

Is there any thing too hard for me? . . .

I needed these words of hope and promise, for by now I knew that in the crash Bobbie's spine had been crushed. If she lived she would be a quadriplegic, not expected to regain the use of muscles below her neck.

As soon as my own broken bones were in casts I was helped down the corridor to Bobbie's room, where she lay strapped to a Stryker frame that rotated her body every hour. She was in too much pain for me to tell her in detail about the spiritual changes in my life. I could only stand in the doorway saying over and over, "God loves you, Bobbie. And I love you."

The kids had been staying at their grandparents' since the crash and that's where I went too, after my discharge. I was supposed to stay in bed, but that first Sunday out of the hospital I asked my aunt to drive me to church. I couldn't wait to learn more about the Immensity that had met me in a six-by-three cubicle. The Law that governed galaxies had turned out to be a very personal Love as well.

When she could be moved, Bobbie was taken to Chicago, where bone from her leg was used to fuse a crushed neck vertebra. The touch-and-go surgery was successful in restoring movement to her arms. A month later she entered a rehabilitation center to learn the skills of living in a wheelchair.

A year after the accident Bobbie came back to a changed home. The special doors and access ramps were only the external alterations. Far more profound were the changes inside ourselves. Having come so close to death, every day of life is for both of us an inexpressible miracle. Time with Bobbie—to talk, to laugh, to hold hands—is far too important for me to crowd my schedule with mere business.

I had time with my children too in the years before they went off to college. In the months while Bobbie struggled for life and strength, I prayed with them for the first time. And when they said, "Do we have to go to church today?" I was the one who said, "Yes."

It wasn't in law school, I told them, that I learned the things that mattered, but in a circle of little red chairs.

HE

Utters

HIS VOICE

Whether you turn to the right or to the left, your ears will hear a voice behind you, saying, 'This is the way; walk in it.' "

—ISAIAH 30:21, NIV

God is our refuge and strength, a very present help in trouble. . . . The heathen raged, the kingdoms were moved; he uttered his voice, the earth melted. The Lord of hosts is with us.

—PSALM 46:1, 6–7

FOUR BIG LITTLE WORDS
—Ivar Seger

Trust in the Lord for His promise is true,
Delight in the Lord, it will bring joy to you.
Commit yourself, do His will every day,
Wait on the Lord, hear what He has to say.

GOD DOES SPEAK TO US
Marion Bond West

Of course, God doesn't tap you on the shoulder and exhort you like your boss, in deep, commanding tones. No, He makes Himself known in various ways. Here's how I came to learn to make myself available to Him.

I never wanted anything in life but to be a wife and mother. I believed this was my calling. When I married Jerry, it all came true for me. By 1968 I was the mother of two young girls and infant twin boys. All four were active and demanding. Suddenly I was up to my ears in diapers and formula and laundry; some days I was so harried and dragged out I never got out of my bathrobe.

Jerry and I were both believers, and when I got the children dressed and we trooped off to church each Sunday, we looked like a picture-book family. We were, except for me. I was drained—running on empty. I began to resent that Jerry went off to work all week to an interesting job with people he enjoyed while I endured daily bedlam at home.

On the morning of March 4, 1972, I told Jerry, "I've got to be alone for a while. Please take the children."

"Sure, sure," he said brightly. "I understand. Maybe it'll cheer you up."

"That's easy for you to say," I said through clenched teeth. Jerry got the message. He quickly collected the children and packed them outside to the yard. It's fortunate he did or I might have screamed at him. I was screaming inside.

I felt like a failure as a wife, mother, and person. I went into the den, shut the door, and whimpered, "Help. Lord, please help me. Take over, I can't do it anymore. There's got to be something more for me in life."

I stood stock still. I wasn't absolutely sure what I was doing. But I listened. Oh, how I *listened.*

And then I began to feel something, a feeling of warmth. I felt a love so intense that it seemed to fill and overflow me and permeate the den and reverberate throughout the whole house . . .

I didn't need to hear words; I could sense Jesus saying, *I've waited a long time for you to do this. I'm pleased and I'm going to help you. I love you.* Although I didn't see anything visible, I knew that Jesus was with me now in a way that He'd never been before, and I felt He was smiling. I smiled back. I'd almost forgotten how to smile. I wondered how I had sung "And He walks with me, and He talks with me, and He tells me I am His own"* almost all my life at church and never once heard Him "say" anything to me before.

Shortly after that experience, I began thinking more and more about my writing—maybe I should write a book. The idea kept returning. Could it be that God was instructing me to write a book?

"I can't," I told Him. "I don't have the time or energy or know-how. I have four small children. I can't even spell. You know how tired I am after the children are asleep. My typewriter is ancient. I want to, but . . . Tell you what, Lord. You know that nice editor lady at *Guideposts* who writes me the encouraging rejection letters, Dina Donohue? Well, if she were to write in her next letter (if there is another letter) 'Dear Marion' instead of 'Dear Mrs. West,' I'd know You were speaking and telling me to write a book . . . and I'd do it."

A letter from Dina Donohue (another rejection) arrived that week. I was standing at our mailbox waiting and looking for it. I read it still standing by the box: "Dear Marion, I cannot call you Mrs. West any longer, for I know you far too well." I

---

*"In The Garden," by C. Austin Miles, © 1912, 1940 by the Rodeheaver Company.

laughed, cried, jumped up and down in the yard, and ran around in a joyful circle as my astonished children gaped.

"God wants me to write a book!" I fairly screamed to them and the neighbors. No one in the world, no theology, no argument, no logic could have convinced me that The God of the Universe had not spoken directly to *me!* It was a long road, but my first book was published four years later.

Sometimes, even as I have learned to listen for God's voice ("My soul, wait thou only upon God," Psalm 62:5), there have been long, dark, almost unbearable times when He didn't speak—or at least I didn't hear Him. When discouraging silence prevailed, I learned that there were always such verses as John 14:18: "I will not leave you comfortless," and Psalm 147:3: "He heals the brokenhearted" (RSV), and many more definite promises. I had to *choose* to stand on them and *believe* them no matter what—as if they were being written for me today.

Once when I was having trouble connecting with God, I asked Him, "Why is it so difficult?" No answer came. Months passed. One night I picked up a book to get my mind off the threatening depression I sensed I'd be facing the next day. Then five words by Oswald Chambers suddenly seemed almost to leave the printed page and invade my defeated spirit like a conquering army rushing to the rescue: "All noble things are difficult."** I sat straight up in bed reasoning: *If all noble things are difficult . . . then I must be doing something noble!* Almost instantly the suffocating depression was lifting. But then I thought, *Why get so excited over five words? Millions of people read this book.* I tuned this out. Belief is for those who want to believe. I had heard from God. I went to sleep savoring, rejoicing in those five words.

Shortly after I began "hearing" from God, Jerry's and my old argument about breakfast resurfaced. Or maybe it was I who argued. Jerry only asked that I cook breakfast, but I hated messing up the kitchen early in the morning. One night after my prayers but before drifting off to sleep, I sensed the words *Cook breakfast for your husband* flashing across my mind.

**My Utmost for His Highest,* by Oswald Chambers, © 1935 by Dodd, Mead & Company.

When I turned to Jerry I saw he was still awake, so I told him, "Jerry, I'm cooking you a good breakfast in the morning." He was so excited that he woke up all during the night wanting to know if it was morning yet. That dutiful obedience put a longed-for new spark in our marriage. Over breakfast Jerry looked at me as if we were dating again. Blessings always follow obedience.

So many times I haven't understood at all why God "told" me to do something, except in retrospect. At another low point in my life God seemed to be telling me to help a quadriplegic: *Teach him to paint.*

"Look," I said, "I can barely paint myself. How can I teach him?" I protested all the way to the hospital where I did volunteer work. When I got to the man's room, he was strapped on a Stryker frame, face down, with his back to me. *This is absurd,* I thought, but I did as God told me and said to the back of his head, "Hi, would you like to learn to paint?"

"Yep. When do we start?" That was in the days before Joni Eareckson had made mouth painting a nationally known technique. I had nothing to go on except instructions from God. The young man began to paint marvelous pictures with a brush held in his teeth. They were framed free of charge by a businessman who recognized his talent. An article about him appeared in the paper. He learned to type by tapping keys with a wand held in his teeth, and went on to lead a full life. How could I stay depressed after I had witnessed a young man make a new life for himself like that?

God's voice is gentle, never pushy. Even when He spoke to me years ago as I stood frying chicken for supper and a dangerous situation was at hand, His voice was calm. I kept "hearing," *Go find your boys. Now.* Finally, I went, hands still covered in flour, to look for them. I thought, *How silly to stop cooking just to look for the boys.* I found Jon and Jeremy in the washroom. Jeremy was crouched in the dryer with the door shut, wearing a space helmet. Jon was about to blast him off into outer space by pushing the "on" button.

There have been times when I've misunderstood God's messages. But even the biblical Samuel missed God's voice a couple of times. However, Samuel was willing to learn to listen. The third time God spoke to Samuel, he answered, "Speak, Lord; for thy servant heareth" (1 Samuel 3:9). I think God just wants us to be willing to learn to *listen* and that He is pleased when we fully *expect* Him to speak. John 10:27 says, "My sheep hear my voice, and I know them, and they follow me," and in Isaiah 30:21 it says, "And thine ears shall hear a word behind thee, saying, This is the way, walk ye in it." Ezekiel 12:25 says, "For I am the Lord: I will speak." I believe God likes to speak. But there are times when I goof. I blow it. Later, when I realize my mistake, I confess, "I'm sorry, Father. Forgive me. I was wrong."

It's all right, child. I know you want to hear from Me. That's all I want. Keep listening. Expecting Me to speak. Don't tune Me out. You are making remarkable progress. I long to tell you so much more.

"Speak, Lord, for Thy servant is listening."

 ## "THE POOR OLD STRANDED WRECK"

Arthur Gordon

Many summers ago, when I was a youngster growing up in Georgia, we had a cottage at the beach. Life there was pretty casual: no church of our denomination, no TV, no radio. So after supper on Sunday nights we had a family custom of singing hymns.

I hadn't thought of this for years, until the other day when my friend Andrew came back from a trip to California. "Met a fellow out there," he said, "who asked me to give you a message. His name was Charlie and he said he used to be a friend of yours. His message was just one word: Thanks."

"Sure," I said, "I remember Charlie. His family had a cottage near ours at the beach. But what was he thanking me for?"

"Well," Andy said, "Charlie remembers singing hymns at your house on Sunday nights. And he remembers one in particular about shipwrecks."

"Yes," I said, a bit surprised, "there was an old hymn called 'Pull for the Shore, Sailor.' "

"Some years ago Charlie got into trouble with alcohol. Big trouble. He lost his job, lost just about everything. Then one night, sitting in a bar, he heard a voice speak to him. He looked all around, but no one was nearby. First the voice called his name. Then it said, strong and clear, 'Leave the poor old stranded wreck, and pull for the shore!' Charlie sat up straight. He was hearing a command. He got up and walked out of the bar and hasn't touched liquor since. He knew who the stranded wreck was."

 ## WITHOUT KNOWING WHY
Shirley and Terry Law as told to Elizabeth Sherrill

Shirley's story:
The orange juice was already poured, the oatmeal nearly cooked, and I was stirring the scrambled eggs, when the crazy thought popped into my mind.

Take the kids to breakfast at McDonald's.

At first I ignored it. I'd been warned by other young widows that your mind plays tricks on you, living alone. I hadn't really been alone since my husband's death in April 1984, six months earlier—but the children were only six and four.

Go to McDonald's.

The thought came more urgently, and for a second I wondered if I was cracking up. But surely the time for that would have been those two-and-a-half years of watching my tall, blond, athletic young husband die inch by inch of a brain tumor.

If grief hadn't been able to destroy my sanity, I thought, mainly to keep my mind off this silly McDonald's notion, money worries might have. Jim had been a stockbroker here in Tulsa, Oklahoma, operating on commission, which stopped when he could no longer work.

I'd found a job selling Visa and MasterCard services to Tulsa businesses. It kept me out in the car a lot, and I'd cried a lot, there in the car. If I'd been going to fall apart, that would surely have been the time, with everything seemingly against us. Even the washing machine broke down, with no money to repair it, so that in the evening after working and cooking and caring for Jim and mowing the lawn, I'd have to drive out to the Laundromat.

Without faith in God, I thought as I gave the eggs a final turn, I really might have gone crazy. I'd carried a Bible in the car; when I felt panic rise I'd pull over and read and pray until I could go on.

The oatmeal was ready too. In the living room the kids were watching the Saturday morning cartoons. "Marie! Jason!" I called. "Wash your hands and come to the table."

And still something inside my head, quite independent of my own thoughts, was insisting that we were to leave this good hot meal right where it was, get in the car, and drive a mile away to a fast food outlet. I'd never in my life eaten breakfast at McDonald's! Where could such a notion be coming from?

Where indeed . . . ? From the bathroom I heard Marie and Jason splashing water on the floor. I stood there at the stove, spatula in hand, thinking back to a chill December day almost two years before. Wondering if the nudging in my head now was in any way like the nudging that had come to me then . . .

For a week I had been giving Jim and the children cold cereal because the stove, like the washing machine, had broken down, and Jim could no longer trust himself to try electrical repairs. We were three months behind on the house payments, and as for Christmas—Santa just wasn't going to find our chimney.

All that winter morning I had called on potential clients without success. As always when our situation threatened to overwhelm me, I'd pulled the car to the side of the road. And there God spoke to me as clearly as though He'd used audible words: *Will you trust Me, Shirley? For Jim, for the children, now and forever?*

I wanted to—oh, how I wanted to! But where could I get that kind of faith? Certainly I couldn't work it up on my own. "Father," I whispered, "give me that trust."

At once a kind of peace seemed to enter the car. And into that peace dropped the names of three local restaurants. I called on all of them that afternoon and signed on three new accounts.

From then on, these "impressions" came often, sometimes

about work, sometimes about Jim's medication or about one of
the children, until I learned to recognize them by a quality of
loving urgency very unlike my ordinary thinking process.

This idea in my head now—if it had been anything except
"Go to McDonald's," I would have said this was one of those
times. But that was too ridiculous!

Wasn't it?

Marie and Jason scrambled into their chairs, still in pajamas
on this one morning of the week when we could loaf around the
house. Well, we could go to the drive-through window . . .

"Get your bathrobes on," I told them. "We're going to bring
breakfast home from McDonald's."

"Yay!" shouted four-year-old Jason. "Can we get French
fries?"

But Marie, two years older, looked from the waiting food to
me, her face as bewildered as I felt.

Not the drive-through. Go inside to eat.

"On second thought," I called as the kids headed for their
rooms, "let's put our clothes on and eat there."

"Boy," I heard Marie tell her brother, "does Mommy ever
change her mind."

Twenty minutes later I was steering through Tulsa's Saturday
traffic, as baffled as ever as to why we were doing this, when
Marie burst into tears. "McDonald's makes me think of Daddy," she sobbed.

Jason was too young to remember the days when Jim could
still drive and used to take the two of them out. But he wasn't
too young to understand sorrow. "Don't cry, Marie," he said.

"Why don't we pray about it?" I interrupted. So we did, and
then Marie said, "God's going to give us a new daddy."

"And someone who loves God," added Jason.

I said nothing. Not out loud. But inwardly I was crying, *No!*
No one could replace Jim. Not ever. It wasn't that I was
mourning, exactly. I'd done that during the years of seizures
and pain. Death had come as such a release for Jim that I'd had
to release him too. It was just that I wasn't ready to open again
to that kind of total involvement.

Before he died, Jim had asked me to remarry. "You're young,
Shirley. You have your whole life ahead of you. Promise me
you'll find someone else—when I'm gone."

But I don't want "someone else"! I protested inwardly as I pulled into the crowded McDonald's lot.

As I'd feared, on a Saturday morning there were long lines at the counter. Thinking ruefully of the eggs congealing in the skillet at home, I inched forward while the kids raced around the playground outside. At last I carried our trays to a window table.

That's where we were sitting when they came in, a stocky curly-haired man with a round, pleasant face—probably in his early forties—and three children, ages maybe twelve to five. I recognized the father at once: Terry Law, director of a singing group I'd seen on Oral Roberts's TV program. Certainly no one I knew personally. And yet . . . the unmistakable "impression" came as I watched the four of them get into line at the counter:

This is the reason you are here.

These four people! This particular group, of all the parents and children jamming the restaurant at this moment?

I went on eating, but the food stuck in my throat. Two years' experience in trusting God was insisting, *Introduce yourself.* When I looked up they were setting their trays down at the very next table.

Lord, I objected silently, *he doesn't know me! I can't just say, "Hello, I'm Shirley."*

Then I remembered that a girl I'd known when I was growing up back in Portland, Oregon, had joined Terry Law's music group, Living Sound, several years ago. I could ask Mr. Law about Paula.

He seemed sort of startled to have me speak to him. Paula had married a young man from Living Sound, he said, and together they were pastoring a church in Alaska. He was still looking at me oddly. Probably wondering why I was butting in on the one day he had with his family. More details about his work were coming back to me. Living Sound traveled all over the world, especially behind the Iron Curtain, where young people turned out by the thousands to hear contemporary music with a Christian message. He must hate to have strangers break into his precious time at home.

Just being polite, no doubt, he asked some questions too. When I'd come to Tulsa from Portland, what the kids' names were, what my husband did.

"Jim died last spring," I said. "I'm a widow." Mr. Law set down his coffee container so hard it slopped over. He mopped it up quickly, said he was sorry about Jim, and wrote down my phone number to give to a lawyer he thought could be helpful. Then with an apology he turned back to the youngsters who were clamoring for his attention.

What in the world, I wondered as Marie and Jason and I went out to our car, had flustered him so? And what, for that matter, I thought as I cleared away the cold remains of our uneaten breakfast back at home, had this whole strange episode of dashing out to McDonald's been all about?

I wasn't really expecting God to tell me. I'd learned to trust Him these past two years, not to understand Him. The trusting is everything: it's peace and joy and security long before the answers come. We see only a step at a time, so He can't usually tell us why.

Except that, in this case, He did . . .

Terry's story:

The conversation with Don Moen occurred on a Monday. Don was music director of our organization, Living Sound, and as usual he and I were aboard an airplane. This particular September day in 1984 we were returning from Arizona to our base in Tulsa, Oklahoma.

Our "base"—that's how I thought of Tulsa now: the place we traveled from. Not "home," not since my wife, Jan, died, even though our three beautiful kids were there, and my mother, who'd come down from Canada to care for Misty and Scot and Rebecca.

Across the aisle of the airplane, Don was watching me. "It's two years this month, Terry," he said, as though reading my thoughts.

Two years since my world had changed in as long as it takes for a car to leave the road and crash into a ditch. I'd been far away in England when it happened. No one ever knew what caused the accident. Perhaps the afternoon sun was directly in Jan's eyes on that east-west Oklahoma road.

I only knew that my life seemed to have ended along with hers. I plunged into a bottomless despair, unable to pray or work or believe that I would ever do these things again.

It was in this mood that I went to see my friend and mentor Oral Roberts. Three months before I lost Jan, Oral had lost a son. "How do you keep going?" I asked him.

"I do it," he said, "by praising God."

Praise? When everything in me wanted to cry and curse? "I didn't say feel it," Oral said. "It is simply a fact that God is very great. Tell Him so."

As Oral predicted, praise was the road back into life. Hollow and mechanical at first, it soon became genuine. Praise for Jan. For the thirteen years we'd had together. For her faith. For knowing for sure that she was right now with Jesus.

Week by week the praise grew stronger—and so did my ability to do the things which at first had seemed impossible: to make plans, to travel, to minister to others around the world. Only the loneliness did not change. Praise helped me to live with the emptiness; it did not fill it.

Friends asked, of course, if I would consider marrying again. I knew I should, for the kids' sake. Eleven, nine, and four— how much they needed a mother!

I knew I should consider it for my mom's sake too. No one could have stepped in more selflessly than she had. But she'd raised her family. In justice she should be taking it easy now.

And yet . . . to consider marrying was just what I could not do. Every time I took my loneliness to God, He seemed to tell me: *two years*. It was always the same. I was not even to let the subject enter my head before that time. And that's what I'd told these friends.

Don was leaning across the narrow airplane aisle. "Two years," he repeated. "Remember what you said?"

"That I couldn't think about marrying for two years," I said. "And I haven't."

"Well, two years are up," Don persisted. "You'd better start thinking."

I leaned my head back in the seat, turning over my not-very-hopeful position. To me my three children were the greatest in the world, but what woman would want to take on marriage and motherhood all at once?

Where, for that matter, would I even meet an unmarried woman my own age? There were plenty of single girls in Living Sound, but they were kids in their twenties. I was forty-one.

I'd want someone I could talk to. Someone who could understand the trauma that Misty and Scot and Rebecca had gone
through.

I kept waiting for Don to pick up a magazine or something,
but from the other side of the aisle he was regarding me
expectantly.

"She'd have to be a widow," I heard myself say. "Someone
who had as good a marriage as Jan and I had, and knows what it
is to lose the most important person in your life. Anyhow,"
I finished, embarrassed at this outburst, "I don't know any
widows."

"God does," Don said. "Let's pray about it."

"I will," I promised him, trying to close off a subject I wasn't
ready for.

But Don had bowed his head. "Father, You know Terry's
need, and his children's need. We believe You have a plan
already at work . . ."

I glanced self-consciously at the other passengers. "Father," I
joined in, keeping my voice as low as I could, "there's a widow
somewhere who—"

"There's a widow in *Tulsa*," Don corrected.

"All right. In Tulsa. I ask that in Your own time—"

"Quickly."

"Okay. I ask that You quickly reveal . . ."

We prayed for several minutes, there on opposite sides of the
aisle, I in generalities, Don in specifics. At the close, he stuck
out his hand. With another nervous glance around, I reached
across and gripped it.

"Thank You, Father," he pronounced, "that it's done."

Just like that. Prayer, in Don's view, didn't have to be long
and eloquent. Just concrete and totally trusting.

At the office in Tulsa a number of crises were waiting for us.
Living Sound had teams on the road both in the United States
and Europe, including several Iron Curtain countries, and the
week was hectic.

Crises or no, however, Saturdays belonged to the family. This
was the morning, when I was home, that I took the kids out to
breakfast. And the outing always started with a debate.

"Grandy's," I suggested as we piled into the car, naming the
place that made the pancakes I liked.

"Denny's," thirteen-year-old Misty voted.

"McDonald's," said six-year-old Rebecca.

"You just like the slide," Scot scoffed with the sophistication of just-turned-eleven. "I say Denny's."

"Denny's wins!" cried Misty.

"Now wait a minute, you two," I said. "Rebecca hasn't gotten to choose for weeks. Let's let her decide today."

And that was how, a few minutes later, the four of us were standing in the line at the McDonald's counter and I was gazing across the room at one of the most beautiful women I'd ever seen. Not a brunette beauty like Jan. This girl had hair the color of sunlight. In fact, where she sat at the window with two little tow-headed kids, the sun streaming through her long blond curls seemed to light up the room.

Maybe it was because I hadn't thought about marriage at all for two years, but I felt a stab of envy for her husband. I was thinking that it would be great just to sit near someone that pretty when, as we left the counter with our trays, the table next to her opened up.

I was trying to decide how to strike up a conversation when to my surprise she did it for me: "Aren't you Terry Law?" A friend of hers, it turned out, had sung for a while with Living Sound. We talked about her friend and then about anything I could think of. I found out that her kids were named Marie and Jason. Their mother's voice was as nice to listen to as her face was to look at.

I peeled the lid from my coffee container as I thought of more questions. Like, "What does your husband do?"

When the girl with golden hair said, "I'm a widow," I took a swallow that scalded my throat all the way down.

What else I said to her I can't remember, except that I managed to get her phone number with some excuse about a lawyer. All I could hear was Don Moen's prayer on the airplane only five days earlier.

All I could think was, *O Lord my God, You are very great.*

Editor's Note: Shirley and Terry were married in January 1985, five months after the "chance" meeting at McDonald's. A sixth child, Laurie Ann Law, was born in March 1986, "but she's not 'ours' any more than all the rest."

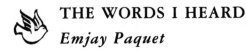

ANSWERS
—*Helen Inwood*

Answers to prayers
Come in various ways,
Sometimes in minutes,
Sometimes in days.
And some take years
To fully unfold
The harvest of love
And blessings they hold.

Answers to prayers
Come in various forms,
Sometimes in sunlight,
Sometimes through storms.
Some blossom early
And some blossom late
But each one will flower—
Have faith and wait!

THE WORDS I HEARD
Emjay Paquet

By the summer of 1977, my heavy drinking had taken its toll. I
was alone, and the only creature in the world that I cared about
was my Burmese cat, Chocolate Mousse. One July day I had
locked myself out of my apartment. The neighbor who helped
me get in not only dried my boozy tears, but went on to tell me
how his own life as an alcoholic had been filled with such
blunders, and tragedy as well. When he finished, I agreed to go
with him on Saturday to get help.

By Friday night, though, I had decided not to go. As I sat
down for a typical evening of bourbon and TV, I began to watch
the film *Days of Wine and Roses*, the story of a marriage between
alcoholics, played by Jack Lemmon and Lee Remick. In one

scene, Jack Klugman, who plays a recovering alcoholic, told Lemmon what would happen if he kept drinking. Klugman slammed his fist on a table and yelled, "Nothing will have any meaning for you anymore—nothing, NOTHING!"

At that point I had a terrible flashback of when, in a drunken rage, a friend had picked up her beloved puppy and hurled him across the room. I looked at my cat. I became afraid that I might even hurt Mousse. I knew then I had to accept my neighbor's offer.

I did, and by the grace of God I've been sober for twelve years. Not long ago I watched that film again, and I waited for the all-important scene between Klugman and Lemmon. This time, though, there was just a conversation, one man explaining alcoholic progression to another. No banging on tables, no one shouting, "Nothing will have any meaning for you anymore." The words that changed my life had never been spoken.

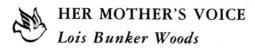

HER MOTHER'S VOICE
Lois Bunker Woods

The year is 1939. The place is an eighty-acre dairy farm outside the small town of Chehalis, Washington, sixteen miles from the nearest doctor or hospital. A little girl, an eighteen-month-old toddler dressed in overalls, slams the screen door as she ambles out onto the back porch to play in the sunshine. Her mother is inside the house, cleaning.

Outdoors on this warm spring morning the world is full of delights to explore. The youngster runs through the dewy grass, picks dandelions, and carries them back to the house. On the porch an old enameled kettle sitting in the sun catches her eye. It is filled with peas soaking in an arsenic solution, something that will prevent them from rotting when planted. Back then, seeds weren't pretreated as most are today.

The little girl is fascinated with the liquid in the kettle. Taking a battered tin cup, she dips it in the pot, fills it with the liquid, then lifts it.

Just then her mother hears a voice calling her, "Ella, Ella,

come quick!" She follows the voice through the house and out
the back door where she spots the little girl, the cup at her lips.
Frantic, she grabs the toddler and empties the cup. She wipes
the little girl's lips, but, no, the youngster hasn't had a drop of
the poison. The mother arrived just in time.

I know this story well because I was that little girl, and the
woman who rescued me was my mother. And as for the voice,
Mother recognized it right away. It belonged to her mother, my
grandmother. The mystery? My grandmother had died the year
before, six months after I was born.

THE SEA ON MY BACK
George Plume

Every submariner lives with one terrifying fear: in a life-or-
death situation he might have to shut the hatch or close a
watertight door on shipmates, thus abandoning them to
death—or even suffer the same fate himself. It is something
you accept and never think about.

Certainly I wasn't thinking about it as the submarine USS
Harder surged smoothly through that night in 1944. It was a
routine evening on war patrol.

Yet, after almost twenty years I can still see that night, hear
it, feel it . . . even smell it.

It was the night I *knew* there was a God—the night I
experienced His real *power* and felt the indescribable wonder of
His presence.

We were slipping along at ten knots, using the hours of
darkness to recharge our batteries and air banks while patrolling
on the surface. Lieutenant Sam Logan, a lanky whiz of a submarine officer, was the Officer of the Day on the bridge. The
second section had relieved the watch at 2000 hours (8:00 P.M.)
and I had taken over as quartermaster on watch.

The lookouts changed at staggered intervals, to prevent clog-
ging the hatchway in the event the bridge watch had to come
scrambling down. There was a man coming and going every
half hour. Up through the control room hatch, turn, two steps

over to the bridge ladder and up, using the dogwheel on the open hatch cover as a handle to pull themselves through the manhole.

On diving, the last man off deck yanks a lanyard that brings the cover slamming down. The quartermaster must then reach up and swiftly spin the dogwheel to extend the dog levers under the hatch rim into locking position.

Except for scattered rain squalls, visibility was good that night. With the enemy coast only an hour's flying time away, our lookouts were "keeping their binoculars warm."

I had just come back down into the conning tower after a topside look around when a low-flying Japanese patrol bomber burst out of a rain squall directly behind us, roaring in for the kill.

The after-lookout screamed the warning, "Clear the bridge!"

The three lookouts came tumbling down the hatch. As quartermaster on duty I leaped for the forward corner to be ready to help Logan secure the cover.

"Dive! Dive!" bellowed through the speakers. Down came Logan, lanyard in fist, pulling the hatchcover closed.

"He's right on top of us!" Logan panted.

Then he swiveled his head and shouted to the control room, "Take her deep . . . FAST!"

With the trip latch apparently engaged, Logan spun away to jump down the control room ladder and take over the dive. There wasn't *time* to wait for a "green board" signal below, which would signify all hull openings closed. Thirty seconds from the diving alarm our decks had plunged beneath the surface.

In those thirty seconds my surprise at the suddenness of the bomber attack turned to utter shock as water poured down upon me from the partially closed hatch. It was stuck and would not close.

I gripped the wheel desperately, twisting back and forth with all my strength, but it was immovable. Fighting water that all but blinded me, I looked over my left shoulder frantically. The helmsman had gone below, right behind Lt. Logan. I was alone.

There was a wild shout from below: "We still got a red light on the bridge hatch!"

But I couldn't answer. The descending water was a fierce torrent and I was choking as I kept up my maddened twisting and jerking at the dogwheel. Roaring in my ears, the terrible noise of the in-rushing sea increased.

A thunderous explosion sledgehammered the hull, then another, causing the *Harder* to jump convulsively. The submarine lurched sideways under the smashing blow of a third Japanese depth charge.

Then, over all the terrifying noise, I heard a heavy clang as the control room hatch slammed shut below. They had abandoned me!

Surfacing, to stop the uncontrollable flooding and save me, meant destruction for the *Harder* and death for every man on board. But I didn't think of that. I didn't think of anything. I tried to scream for help. And then I went berserk as I wrenched and tore at that jammed dogwheel. All *I* knew was that I didn't want to die—not alone in here—like this. The awful force above tore me away from the hatch mechanism, while inexorably from below, the water rose in that tiny, steel cubicle. I grabbed for the ladder . . .

I was paralyzed by fear beyond description, a miserable fright born of complete helplessness. Yet, deep within me was the recurring thought *God help me, God help me.* It was not an uttered or conscious prayer. My panic had carried me past such intelligence. I couldn't fight, I couldn't think. I couldn't *ask* for God's intervention.

And that is when it happened.

Suddenly, through the chaos, there came a quieting and a strange feeling of reassurance. It seemed, inexplicably, that in the few moments I had left there was plenty of time. Then from the calm within me came these words, which I shall hear for the rest of my days: "George, *open the hatch!*"

Without question or thought, obediently, and with strength that had left my body, I reached up. This time I turned the dogwheel *back,* to open the hatch. The dogs stuck for a heartbeat then slid back, easily . . . and the monstrous sea pressure immediately pressed the hatch tight on the rim! Instantly the crushing downpour dwindled to a trickle.

Methodically, I slowly reversed the wheel and secured the hatch. The trickle stopped. I turned to look about me in wonder. Then I forged through the water to get my hand on the speaker "talk" lever and said, "It's okay. The hatch is closed. You can pump this place out now."

I've marveled for years, in thinking back, that even then, without conscious thought I did *not* say, "I closed the hatch." The truth bespoke itself. The hatch *was* closed, but not by me.

The conning tower was pumped out, the hatch below opened, and I climbed down to rejoin my back-pounding, joyful shipmates. Commander Sam Dealey, one of the finest men I shall ever know, had quiet words of commendation as the boat cruised safely in the depths.

But through all of it there was that one question . . . that single, small, lingering doubt. I turned to Lt. Logan and asked, "Did anybody down here use the speaker to tell me to open the hatch?" The looks of surprise around the control room told me what I guess I already knew. Someone else had helped me.

Today, almost twenty years later, I still feel the mighty power of that reassurance—that He is a practical, ever-present God, that He has a plan for each of us. And in that knowledge I have a serene, indestructible, immovable faith that I, simply, humbly, and gratefully, try to share with those about me.

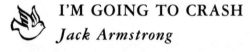

I'M GOING TO CRASH
Jack Armstrong

Things weren't going as I had expected that blustery March night in 1972 over Arkansas.

I was flying a single-engine four-seat Cherokee 180 from Chicago for delivery to Houston and had planned to reach Shreveport, Louisiana, that night. But as I passed over Fort Smith, Arkansas, I recomputed my ground speed and found that I was pushing into a head wind of much greater velocity than had been forecast. That meant I would not have enough fuel to reach Shreveport.

It was 8:00 P.M. A light rain beat against my windshield like scatter shot and a heavy overcast blocked out any moonlight. Even at my assigned altitude of seven thousand feet, I couldn't see a thing; it was pitch black outside my cockpit windows. Instrument weather.

No problem, though. Over my radio I requested clearance to land at nearby Texarkana, Arkansas.

Texarkana approach control came on clear: "Okay, Cherokee seven-nine-four-eight-n, descend and maintain two thousand feet; you are cleared for an instrument approach to the airport."

I settled back. I enjoyed these flights. Ever since I got out of the Navy in 1971, flying had been my main goal in life. And I was doing all right with it. I figured I could take care of myself.

I finished my landing check list and, by instrument check, found my position to be about thirty miles north-northwest of the Texarkana airport. I knew that a thick forest of pine trees and rolling hills were beneath me.

Suddenly my engine coughed, quit . . . started . . . and quit again! What was wrong? Frantically I checked instruments. There was plenty of fuel. I pushed controls, checked again. Nothing. A cold fear seized me.

Now only wind noise filled the cockpit as my 2450-pound plane began its inexorable drop to earth. I sat helpless at the dead controls as my ship hurtled into the total blackness. Terror shot through me as I thought of smashing into the thick pines that would tear my ship to shreds.

I began a series of emergency measures. I radioed a Mayday distress call to the air controller, advising him of my situation. Then I set the Cherokee into a glide speed of eighty miles an hour, extended-ten degree flaps, and noted that we were dropping 1100 feet per minute. That meant less than two minutes before we would crash. I still could not see anything outside the windows.

I then did the only other thing I could do. "O Lord Jesus," I prayed, "into Your hands I come."

Suddenly, unbelievably, a complete peace filled the cabin. Fear left me. In its place I felt a strange presence. Words seemed to fill my mind—words of calm and reassurance. *Everything is going to be all right. Look off your left wing.*

Then, through a clear spot in the murky skies, I saw a light from a house porch. Instinctively I swung the plane toward it.

Again the Voice in my mind. *Now look below to your right.*

When I looked, I saw the headlights of two cars coming toward me.

Head directly for those two cars; everything is going to be all right.

The deep indescribable feeling of peace and beauty intensified.

I kept heading toward the headlights; they were the only
thing I could see outside the cockpit. The plane shuddered from
wind gusts as we silently sped downward. I switched on my
landing lights and continued on.

Whoosh! I passed about thirty feet over the first car and was
immediately engulfed by tall dark trees racing close by on both
sides. I sensed I was lined up with the highway, but I seemed to
be flying into a tunnel.

The Voice kept assuring me. *Everything will be all right.*

Now the second car was facing me head-on and I felt sure
we'd collide. I tried to turn the plane, but my hands and legs
would not respond.

Keep heading for that car, continued the soft, soothing Voice.
Everything is going to be all right.

My air speed had dropped drastically; the red stall light was
frantically indicating that there wasn't enough air flow over my
wings to maintain a safe glide.

Then I felt an impulse to do the strangest thing. Despite my
critically low air speed, I was suddenly prompted to pull back
on the controls, raising the plane's nose into a high attitude so
that the lighter tail section would hit the oncoming car first.
Ordinarily such a maneuver would lead to a total stall and crash.
I waited for the impact.

There was none. Instead, the highway pavement appeared in
my landing lights, rising steeply. I was heading uphill! But
because of my high nose attitude, the plane set down on the
concrete in a perfect three-point landing. I rolled to the top of
the hill and began using my brakes. There at the side of the
highway was a roadside café, its neon sign saying "Penney's
Cafe" glowing. I kept using the brakes, rolled into the café's
parking lot and stopped.

Suddenly the immensity of the incredible thing that had
happened overwhelmed me. All I could do was sit there thanking God.

Light flooded the parking lot as the café door opened and a
man walked toward me. "How did you get *here?*" he asked in
astonishment.

"A miracle of God," I said in a choked voice.

I asked the man to check down the road; I was worried about

the people I might have run off the highway. After ten minutes he came back. He had found no one and did not recall seeing any cars earlier.

Were those lights real, I wondered, or had the Lord put them there just for me? All I know is that if I had not lifted my plane's nose to avoid the second car, I certainly would have slammed into the inclined highway. My lights did not shine far enough for me to react to landing uphill. The impact probably would have caused the plane to explode, since I had about fifteen gallons of fuel left in the wing tanks.

There was not a scratch on the plane. The air traffic controllers in Texarkana were amazed to find me alive. What had caused the engine to quit? A clogged fuel line.

I learned that the road I had landed on was U.S. Highway 71. So that night after I checked into a motel, just out of curiosity I picked up the Bible in my room and turned to the 71st psalm. It began, "In thee, O Lord, do I put my trust. Let me never be put to confusion. . . ."

I put the book down and looked out the window. The dark mist was falling and the sky was still black. But I knew that above that overcast the stars were still shining, though I couldn't see them. And now I knew, more certainly than ever before, that the Lord of Heaven was there as well.

I HEARD HIS CRIES
Virginia Ann Van Seters

I'm a sound sleeper. Only thirst or a headache ever wakes me up. A car speeding past, a dog barking, a passing thunderstorm—I can sleep through almost anything. But for no apparent reason I woke up with a start one cool fall night.

At first I thought it was time to get up. No, my clock showed 1:00 A.M. I listened. All was still, yet I felt as though I had awaked for some reason. I sat on the side of the bed, bolt upright. Several minutes passed. The bedroom windows were closed and the curtains drawn. No noise from the outside. There was total silence.

Then I heard, distinctly, a man's voice: "Help me, help me. Oh, please, help me!"

The voice sounded like it was in the room with me. "Help me, help me! Oh, please, help me!"

Immediately I called the police emergency number. "Someone needs help," I said, "out near my street." I told the dispatcher where I lived and, satisfied that I had done all I could, I went back to bed.

Even before I fell asleep, the police dispatcher called me back. She sounded incredulous. "How did you know someone was there?" she asked.

"I heard his cries," I said.

"But how could you?" she asked. She knew my condominium was set well back from the street. My windows were closed and I hadn't heard the police drive by. "The man you heard," she explained, "was trapped in a car at the bottom of a ravine nearly two blocks away."

"I heard him," I said. Somehow I heard him.

 ## UNSCHEDULED APPOINTMENT
Jeanne Murray Hill, R.N.

My flight home from a brief trip to New York had been a pleasant one—up until the last half-hour. Then, for no reason at all, apprehension began to gather in me like the dark clouds of the turbulence we'd just passed through over Texas.

But the turbulence hadn't unnerved me. After fifteen years of being a nurse, it takes a lot to rattle me. That's what was so strange about my unease. When the pilot announced, "We passed through the turbulence easily with only a small time loss," my hand shook so that I spilled my coffee. One thought flashed through my mind like a danger signal: *We'll be late landing in Phoenix.*

Why worry? I asked myself. I wasn't trying to make plane connections. I was just going home. My husband and children would be in no hurry. It had long been a practice in our family to make meeting planes a family-fun occasion. The children enjoyed watching the other planes land before the special plane was met. Then we would always have Cokes together in the airport before going home. So, there was no *reason* to be upset over being a few minutes late, I chided myself. That thought was followed by the warning, *Hurry!*

I looked about me. Who had spoken? Or had I only *felt* someone had spoken? In spite of my protesting logic I folded my blanket and returned it to the rack above the seat. Then I straightened myself and collected all my belongings as if we were on the ground, ready to disembark.

I felt no calmer once my things were collected. In fact, I felt more upset. I glanced at my watch. How ridiculous! Fifteen more minutes. I asked the stewardess for a glass of water and fumbled in my purse for an air-sickness pill. But, as I fingered the white capsule, again I felt it. *No. The pill will relax you. And you will need to hurry!*

But why would I need to hurry? I'd just phoned my family before getting on the plane. They were all well and safe— unless they had had an accident on the way to the airport. No, I was sure that my family was all right. But I didn't take the pill.

For the next fifteen minutes I sat, belongings in hand, waiting to land. Soon below us Phoenix was a glistening canopy of lights in the black night.

"When will we land?" the man behind me asked the stewardess. "Are we very late?"

"Any minute now," she answered, checking her watch. "We'll be about four minutes late." Her words sent a chill through me. *You should be down there now!* But what possible difference could four minutes make?

Yet, I felt it again. *Hurry up. Get out your baggage stubs.* The words were felt more than actually heard, so definite this time that I obeyed without question. The plane landed safely and taxied to the terminal.

When the "fasten your seat belts" sign flashed off, I jumped out of my seat and scrambled down the ramp. I was glad to see my family well and safe. But still that didn't relieve my feeling of anxiety. A stronger force was now guiding my very footsteps. I barely kissed the family, scooped up my four-year-old into my arms, and kept walking. My husband glanced at me questioningly when I headed away from the restaurant, the scene of our usual gab-fest.

"I *need* to get my baggage," I called over the children's heads. They followed me reluctantly toward the baggage depot. There I could see my two blue suitcases, but something else caught my eye!

Three feet in front of my bags was a small cluster of people around a wheelchair. *Hurry up! Go to him! You're late!* I ran to the group and pushed my way through. A man in his sixties lay slumped in the chair. His skin was ashen. "He's got a chronic lung condition, but he's never been this bad before," said the man's wife, her voice shaking.

"I'm a nurse," I said. I examined the man. He wasn't breathing. There was no pulse. I put my ear to his chest; I thought I heard a very faint heartbeat.

"Dear God, help me," I said under my breath, then aloud:

"You! Call an ambulance," I pointed to a young man in the tiny gathering. To another I said, "Call the Fire Rescue Squad."

"Louis," I turned to my husband, "help me get him to the floor."

Once the ill man was flat on the floor, I began mouth-to-mouth resuscitation, alternately blowing, resting, not daring to stop. By the time another nurse, also a passenger, arrived on the scene, an occasional beat of the man's heart could be felt in the pulse at his wrist.

The additional nurse and I were able to massage the heart externally. We continued mouth-to-mouth resuscitation until the Fire Rescue Squad came with an oxygen unit. Then a passing doctor arrived to help us. By now, the ill man's pulse was becoming more and more frequent.

When the ambulance arrived ten minutes later, his color had changed from ashen to life-pink.

My children, who had stayed off to the side, out of the way, joined my husband and me as we watched the ambulance drive off.

"I've got your suitcases, Mom," my son said.

"Thanks," I murmured, and then I said another heartfelt "thanks" to that voice I'd felt—to the One who knew that four minutes made the difference between life and death.

A phone call to the hospital the next day reassured me that the man would fully recover. I've recovered too—recovered my faith that over the years had become so casual I no longer expected the type of guidance that came to me on the airplane.

Yet, I know now that God can speak to us in many ways. He can even nudge us to hurry when He has a job for us.

 ## THE VOICE I DIDN'T WANT TO HEAR
Ingrid Widdell

Whenever I hear people debating whether God really contacts people with specific instructions, my mind goes back to an episode in my own life several years ago. It started in church one Saturday evening in my hometown of Gothenburg (Göteborg), Sweden, a persistent thought that had nothing to do with the service or the sermon but would not let me alone.

Go down to the harbor!

The harbor? At night? Me, a lone woman, go down to the roughest part of town? I impatiently thrust away the idea.

But it would not go. As distinctly as though a voice were pronouncing it I heard again, *I want you to go down to the harbor.*

Suppose it was a message from God Himself? But why would He send me to such a place on a dark and windy October night? I pictured the wet railroad tracks along the wharves, the deserted sheds and huge lonely cranes, the drunks and the prostitutes who roamed the area. And I turned my mind firmly back to the sermon.

It was no good, I couldn't concentrate. Each time the minister paused, that other thought was waiting for me.

"I have work for you to do at the harbor."

I squirmed in my pew until the service ended, then hurried home as fast as I could to put as much distance as possible between myself and this alarming idea. I actually slammed my door when I got inside, and at last the mysterious voice was silent.

But not my conscience. The event had a sort of sharp edge to it. As weeks went by, I could still recall the reality and clarity of that command, and I became more and more convinced that it had, in fact, come from God Himself.

And then suddenly one evening toward the end of November, the voice was back. *Go down to the harbor tonight.*

Near me lived an elderly couple who were members of my church and who, I knew, had had several experiences of divine guidance. Now I went to their house and told them the amazing instruction I seemed to be getting. They seemed to find it neither surprising nor particularly unusual.

"I'm an old fellow," the husband said, "and not much protection, but I'll come along with you anyway." And so the two of us set out.

The harbor in Gothenburg is big and that night there were many vessels in port. Where in all this area were we supposed to go?

We asked God to tell us and right away we had the distinct impression that we were to go on board a freighter.

But what one? Which dock?

The answer we seemed to receive was that we should try boarding the first vessel we came to. If we were refused, this was the wrong one. Eventually we would come to a ship we could walk straight on.

First at the pier before us was a big tanker. A watchman at the gangway looked so formidable that we did not even approach him. When we boarded the next two vessels, watchmen quickly accosted us and asked our business. Twice I opened my mouth to explain about the voice; twice I closed it and backed meekly down the gangplank. Soon we were standing in front of a Scottish freighter, which appeared to be deserted. Still, in obedience to our instructions, we went aboard. On the deck we saw a tiny beam of light coming from beneath a door. Opening it, we found ourselves at the head of a stairway up which came the sound of noisy voices. We went down.

And stepped straight into a wardroom filled with crewmen in all degrees of intoxication. "Welcome!" several thickly cordial voices greeted us. One of the men gallantly swept some bottles aside to make more room at the table. "Sit down! Have a drink!"

We accepted the seat but found declining the drink in our clumsy English a little more difficult. Soon an awkward silence fell over the room. At last there was nothing to do but to blurt out something about docks and voices and a job that maybe God wanted me to do.

Soon I found myself talking as rapidly about God as my
English permitted, and how I had found a new life when I
turned to Him for forgiveness some years ago.

A sound behind me made me turn. In the doorway stood a
tall middle-aged man with a week's growth of beard on his
chin, an empty bottle in one hand, and the filthiest suit of
clothes I'd ever seen.

"Ian . . ." someone muttered. "Come in and sit down." Ian
swayed in and stopped in front of me. Evidently he had been
listening for some time for he burst out: "She's right, she's
right. Don't you think I know . . . but that was long ago . . .
ten dirty black years have gone since I ran away from God."

He leaned against the table as he spoke. Nobody said a word.
He told about the church he had attended, about his wife, his
children, and how he had lost them when he started to drink.
Then something seemed to flash through his brain. He pointed
the bottle at me and shouted:

"I'm that job, Miss! I'm the one God sent you to find!"

My heart was thumping. What on earth should I do now?
The room was silent as the men seemed to ponder all this.

I started to pray silently and then I heard myself saying, "On
Saturday nights we have a service at our church. Will you come
with me, Ian? I will pick you up at eight o'clock."

"I'll be ready," he said.

A few minutes later we said goodbye to the sailors and left.

The rest of the week doubt fought with the hope building in
me. The man had probably forgotten the whole thing by the
next morning! But on Saturday night my old friend and I were
back at the dock. The Scottish vessel was still there. My heart
leaped when Ian came down the gangplank nicely dressed in hat
and overcoat—and sober.

That night Ian sat beside me while I whispered translations of
the Swedish service to him. At the close, when several people
went into another room for prayer, I asked Ian if he, too,
wanted to go. He nodded a silent yes.

We knelt with the others and here this modern prodigal son
experienced his Heavenly Father's forgiveness. When Ian stood
up, you could almost see the inner light radiating from him and
you could sense his new peace of soul.

Five weeks later I was back at the harbor to meet the Scottish
freighter when it anchored. Looking tanned and clear-eyed, Ian

greeted me. He told me he had gone back to his family and asked them to forgive him. "The hardest thing was to face my children. But with God's grace I'll be a father to them yet."

As for his wife, he said, "She told me that never once in all those years did she stop praying for me."

Then I knew how God had answered those prayers. He had followed Ian's ship across the North Sea to give a lost soul another chance. And He had given me a second chance as well. That windy night in October when I first heard and failed to obey that voice, that was the night Ian's ship had first docked in Gothenburg.

HE

Increases

STRENGTH

He gives power to the faint,
   and to him who has no might he increases strength.
. . . .
they who wait for the Lord shall renew their strength,
   they shall mount up with wings like eagles,
they shall run and not be weary,
   they shall walk and not faint.

—ISAIAH 40:29–31, RSV

HE GIVETH MORE GRACE
—*Annie Johnson Flint*

He giveth more grace when the burdens grow greater,
   He sendeth more strength when the labors increase;
To added affliction He addeth His mercy,
   To multiplied trials, His multiplied peace.

When we have exhausted our store of endurance,
   When our strength has failed ere the day is half done,
When we reach the end of our hoarded resources,
   Our Father's full giving is only begun.

His love has no limit, his grace has no measure
   His power has no boundaries known unto men;
For out of his infinite riches in Jesus
   He giveth and giveth and giveth again.

MAMA, COME QUICK
Joan B. Paris

After my grandfather died, my uncle Bill was the only one left living in the old family home with my grandmother. She was ninety-three and he was sixty-five, but they depended on each other like siblings. He'd get the Nashville newspaper every morning and bring her breakfast and keep her up-to-date on the rest of the family.

One morning, though, after twenty-three years of the same routine, he got up at seven o'clock, swung both feet over the side of his bed, and suddenly collapsed to the floor with a stroke. Conscious but unable to move, he yelled to my grandmother in her bedroom, "Mama, Mama!"

"Why are you hollering so early in the morning?" she called back, roused from her sleep.

"Mama," he said, "come quick."

Grandmother knew then that something was terribly wrong. Quickly she called to the One who had never failed to hear her every prayer, then got out of bed. She hurried to my uncle's room, where he lay paralyzed. Knowing help was needed, she telephoned their next-door neighbor and went downstairs to let the neighbor in. Together they went to Bill's room; medical help was summoned and soon arrived.

What was so unusual about this? Wouldn't any mother have done the same? Yes, perhaps. But you see, Grandmother had been permanently injured in a car accident and since then had fallen, breaking her hip twice. She had been in a wheelchair for nine years. During that time she had not taken one step by herself.

SEND SOMEONE . . . ANYONE!
Mildred Shell, as told to Jorunn O. Ricketts

On that sunny August afternoon several years ago, there was no indication that anything could mar the beauty and peace of the day. It was a Friday, and I could hear the hum of my husband's tractor as he mowed the grass in the field next to our backyard.

Our house stands on a hill above the highway about a mile from the little town of Marble Hill, Missouri. Mr. Stephens, a farmer, is our nearest neighbor and he lives a quarter of a mile down the road.

I don't know what it was that caused me to turn suddenly and look at my husband on the tractor. As I did so, I watched in horror and disbelief as the tractor hit something hard in the grass, then turned over, pinning my husband beneath.

In a panic I began running toward the tractor knowing that I had to get Howard out from under before it burst into flames.

Jack, our ten-year-old son, was already by his father's side. Together we pulled and pried, but all our efforts seemed only to hurt Howard, who was lying on his back with the steering wheel pressing against his chest. One of his legs was caught

under the back end of the heavy machine, a Farmall Cut, which
weighed three thousand pounds.

Our cries for help rang out across the empty field. We could
hear the cars go by on the highway, but they couldn't possibly
hear us.

Howard was struggling to breathe—if the weight of the
tractor wasn't lifted off his chest, he might die! Frantically we
searched for something to prop up the tractor. There was
nothing.

O God, I thought in despair, *send someone . . . anyone!*

I didn't stop to think how hopelessly ridiculous it would be for a
woman alone to try to lift a tractor. I only knew that Howard would
die if it wasn't done. With one shoulder leaning against the
radiator, I took hold and lifted with all my might . . . and the
tractor moved. I was holding it up, thank God! Howard was
breathing easier. He was saved, at least for the moment.

"You try and pull Daddy out," I said to Jack. "I'll hold the
tractor."

Jack was pulling as hard as he could, but Howard wasn't
moving.

"I can't." Howard was straining to breathe and talk at the
same time. "A rock . . . under my back . . . I'm hurt." His leg
was still pinned under the tractor. It was obvious that we
couldn't get him out without help.

"Run," I said to Jack. "Phone Mr. Stephens and ask him to
bring help."

I watched Jack race across the yard and into the house and
prayed that our neighbor was at home.

Then, for a while, it was as if time had been suspended. I
didn't seem to be aware of the weight of the tractor and I wasn't
even bothered by the heat. Meanwhile, Howard was struggling
to speak. "I . . . can't . . . take . . . it . . . much . . . longer."

In many private conversations Howard and I had agreed that
death was not something to fear. We had surrendered our lives
to God many years before. Miraculously, we felt, He had
brought Howard back after a head wound nearly killed him on
Saipan during World War II. And now, once again, Howard
was in God's hands. With a sudden calmness I knew that if
Howard was to live, God would use me to hold up the tractor
till help came.

Finally I saw them running toward us—Jack and Mr. Stephens and his son, Jerry, and Henry Thiele, another neighbor. Together they lifted the tractor. The doctor arrived, and then the ambulance. Howard's leg had to be stitched up, and the doctor said X rays would be necessary. "But I don't think he's seriously hurt."

Then Mr. Stephens took my right arm firmly and said, "Now I'll take *you* to the doctor."

"Me, what in the world for?" I could feel no pain anywhere. But then I looked and saw that the skin and flesh of my left arm and shoulder was hanging in shreds. I could hardly believe what I saw. At the clinic the doctor explained that the heat from the radiator had actually cooked the flesh on my arm and shoulder to the bone.

In a few days Howard came home in a wheelchair to nurse a crushed vertebra in his back. My left arm was helpless until the burnt muscles slowly healed. For months we were quite a pair, both semi-invalids with a house and two children to care for.

Every time we think back to that August Friday, we marvel at the way things worked out. When Jack telephoned our neighbor for help, Mr. Stephens just *happened* to walk into his kitchen in time to take the call. His son Jerry, who no longer lives at home, just *happened* to be there visiting that day.

And all the while God was lifting that tractor for almost one hour. I wasn't. On my own I couldn't. We still have the tractor, and I have since tried lifting the front end. I can't budge it.

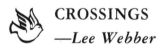 CROSSINGS
—*Lee Webber*

I came to the swift, raging river,
    And the roar held the echo of fear;
"Oh, Lord, give me wings to fly over,
    If You are, as You promised, quite near."

But He said, "Trust the grace I am giving,
    All-pervasive, sufficient for you.
Take My hand—we will face this together;
    But My plan is—not over, but through."

THEY SAY—I RISKED MY LIFE
Harold D. Walters

"If you go through with it, Walters, it may cost you your life," the doctor warned me.

I sat there numbly, slumped down in his office chair. Idly, I picked at the loose thread on my coat button. The words had sunk into my subconscious mind, but as yet I hadn't fully translated them.

"You should go to bed at once to prevent any more hemorrhages. In the very near future we will get you off to a dry climate," the doctor continued. "Can't take chances with tuberculosis."

I got up, put on my top coat, and carefully smoothed out a wrinkle in my hat. I avoided looking again at the sympathy I knew would be in the doctor's face. The air in his office seemed unbearably close and hot.

Outside I paused a moment and looked toward the street. The late afternoon shadow cut directly down the middle of my car, leaving one half a bright orange and the other a drab brown.

"Good afternoon, Mr. Walters." The voice—that of a woman on the sidewalk—came from a thousand miles away. "We're looking forward so much to the performance tomorrow. My two sisters drove all the way from Des Moines to see you play the Christus."

Her words thumped dully against my eardrums. I walked by her to my car, reaching for my key case. Traffic was heavier than usual. People even now were arriving from hundreds of miles away for the final performance of the Passion Play tomorrow. The Scottish Rite Temple Auditorium here in Bloomington, Illinois, would bulge with fifteen hundred of them.

"No it won't," I said, half to myself, half out loud. I had a crazy desire to go out into the street, stop traffic, and tell 'em all to go back home. *Because there wasn't going to be a Passion Play tomorrow.*

Back at home in my study chair, I began to think more coherently. Perhaps it wasn't the end of everything. A few months in New Mexico . . . maybe a year . . . a gradual return to normal health . . . then here again to my insurance business—and the Passion Play. Some of the mist began to clear away.

I made an effort to rise and phone Delmar Darrah, director of the play. Better tell him now and get it over with. But a heavy weight in my chest held me down. Who would he get to understudy? I alone could play Jesus tomorrow. The play would have to be called off.

Bitterness welled up inside me. Why this to me? Had God decided suddenly that I was unworthy to play the role of Jesus?

Then, like a white light ripping into a dark room, came a new thought. *I have lived many glorious hours as Christ, if only in a play.* I had poured my whole being into the part—had tried to think and act like He would. *Right now, in this very room, I will try to be as He would be.* What would Jesus do in my situation? I sat deep in thought for a long time.

Later I arose from the chair, moved over to the telephone, and dialed a number. "Doctor," I said, "I will follow your instructions to the letter—after I do the final presentation tomorrow."

I explained to my family that I was not trying to be melodramatic or heroic and was happy when they agreed even though they were fearful. After quiet meditation the solution had seemed so very simple. The Passion Play was an inspiring, holy masterpiece. Tomorrow it would uplift some fifteen hundred people. It would bring God a little closer to every one of them. This seemed to more than justify any physical danger chanced by one unimportant human being.

The next day I arrived at the auditorium in plenty of time to do a slow careful job on my makeup. I didn't want to be hurried or rushed. Every bit of strength had to be saved for the performance itself.

As I sat in the dressing room, fingering the familiar makeup boxes and sniffing the pungent odor of grease paint, I thought how much I had loved playing this role. This 1940 performance would be my third since I had earned the part in 1938. Many thoughts darted through my head. I suppose it is normal for one who plays the Christus to want to try, regardless of how inadequately, to pattern his life after the Prince of Peace. I had spent much of my time teaching Sunday school and preaching sermons to help spread the gospel. In the Passion Play I had found a way to bring a message to thousands of people far more effectively than from a pulpit. I loved these hours more than anything else in life.

Then I had a sudden spasm in my chest—worse than any before.

The man helping me with my makeup was aghast. Quickly he helped me over to a couch. Then he started to bolt for the door—to tell the others.

I grabbed his coat. "Please?" I shook my head weakly. "I'll be all right in a minute."

"You'll kill yourself!" he protested. But I made him promise not to say anything.

When strength returned, I resumed my makeup. Curtain time was at hand. During final adjustments to my costume I thankfully noted that the dark beard and paint almost completely concealed my pale features.

Before leaving the dressing room, I lowered my head for a moment. "Please, Lord, am I doing Your will, or is it just pride that is driving me on? Let me do what is right." I knew that only with His help and strength would I be able to go through with the performance. I was confident that He would not fail me.

The play opened on schedule at 1:30 P.M. The curtains parted, the light shone from above, and I, as Jesus, was in the opening scene giving the Sermon on the Mount.

At the end of the first scene I was exhausted. Moving about and talking had been torture. The salt taste of blood was in my mouth from internal bleeding.

During the second-scene curtain I had to lie down for a moment. "What's wrong with Walters?" I heard someone ask. "Temperament," a stagehand replied significantly.

I smiled wryly to myself. But at that moment all that mattered to me was whether I could finish. The words of Jesus on the cross never had such sharp meaning—"My God, my God, why hast thou forsaken me?"

In this moment of near collapse I remembered, like a message, a casually made statement by one of the actors who in real life is a linotype operator for Bloomington's only newspaper. "Once a year," he had said, "I have a chance to be John the Disciple, not just Clifton Webb of Bloomington. And for those hours *I am* Disciple John."

Here was my answer. I could not be Harold Walters and ever go through with the rest of the play. I had to forget myself, my pain, my fears, everything *but being Jesus* . . .

Back on the stage I began to lose myself in Him. The tremendous beauty and excitement of the role swept me up. The pain left my chest. My voice grew stronger—clearer. Strength poured into my arms and legs. The moments became sheer splendor. I wanted them to last forever.

When the final curtain went down, I glowed with exhilaration. God had come. He had poured His strength into me. For those sublime moments His divine Spirit had been in me.

When a rest cure of six months in New Mexico ended my illness, I returned to Bloomington at once. It was time to begin preparations for my role of Christus again.

Today I am considered to have an arrested case of tuberculosis. Two years ago I was able to buy more life insurance.

This April 4 (1948) I will play the role of Christus again for the eleventh straight year. Few moments of real bliss come to a man's life. But once each year I have them—during the Passion Play.

I also believe that some time in every person's life comes a real test of faith—some moment when it seems foolhardy, even wrong, to try to follow the Footsteps. I am convinced that no one can ever meet this test alone. It can only be done with the help of God, through prayer, and an uncompromising desire to do His will.

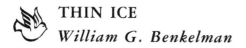

THIN ICE
William G. Benkelman

The temperature had hovered between freezing and zero for almost a week. When I got home from work that Friday in February 1975, I glanced at the frozen Rocky River, just a few feet from our door—and it looked inviting.

"What about having some friends over for skating tonight?" I asked my wife, Sylva. Whenever the ice was good, we liked to floodlight the area behind our house and play skating music on the hi-fi. Afterward skaters would come upstairs for cookies and coffee before a roaring fire in our living room. But this time Sylva said no. She is a registered nurse and she had been working at the hospital since 7:00 A.M., so she was very tired.

The sun was still shining and I figured there would be a good half hour before dark for me to skate. Down the stairs I went and put on my skates on the dock under our house. The ice tested very strong, the temperature was twenty-two degrees, and there was no wind—a great combination. It was exhilarating. At a smooth clip I traveled across the lagoon in back of our house and suddenly felt so invigorated that I decided to skate on—to the river, up the west channel, and around the island on which the Cleveland Yachting Club is located. The club was closed for February; it looked like a ghost town of dry-docked boats.

"Great skating!" I shouted happily to a woman skating with some children, the only people around. I shot ahead, under the little bridge that connected the island to the far bank, on and on until I headed once more into the river, clipping along, now in the middle, a hundred feet from shore, when . . .

Oh, oh—a patch of soft ice. Slush. I thought I could coast through it, but I slowed down. I stroked with my right foot; the ice gave way under it. I tried to stroke with the other, but *it* broke through. I was in trouble. Bad trouble.

Immediately I knew why. It was because of the big bridge high above me. For days the city had been spreading salt on it to melt the snow on the roadbed. The salt had filtered down to the river, softening the wide path of ice I had skated into. Now I found myself sinking through the ice, then suddenly plunging up to my neck in freezing water.

I did not panic. I did not thrash about. I hollered. I pounded away at the mushy ice in an attempt to reach ice firm enough to support me. I knew I had to do something fast, for I had read somewhere that a person can survive only three minutes in freezing water. I was aware, too, of an unusual fact about myself—that I am incapable of floating. I'm so thin, more bones than flesh, that I have what is called negative buoyancy— when I'm not moving my arms or legs in water, I sink to the bottom.

I tried to work myself toward firmer ice by breaking off small pieces along the edge. But it was taking too much time. This way I'd freeze to death before I'd ever get out. I could hear no one answering my cries; the bridge above me was humming with rush-hour traffic, yet I knew, because of the railing and the angle, that no one in a passing car could see me. I simply had to think of another way to get myself out of the water.

Then it came to me. I swim regularly, every week, and it was not unusual for me to swim the length of the "Y" pool underwater. I looked at the shore a hundred feet away and realized that if I could swim that distance under the ice, I could break through at the shore. It was a gamble, but I saw no hope any other way. I took one last look around to see if anyone was in sight. No one. "And if I don't make it," I said to myself, "no one except God will ever know what happened."

There in the water, about to dive under the ice, thinking of God, I felt ashamed before Him. "I'm sorry," I prayed to Him. "I'm sorry I've been so careless with Your precious gift of life. I want to live, God. I want desperately to live, but I'll accept Your will."

In those brief moments I didn't ask God to save my life. It had been a long time since I had asked Him for anything at all. Sylva and I had married in 1953 and, of course, we wanted children. We did everything we could, including a lot of praying, but no children came. After praying for ten years I had come to the conclusion that God wasn't listening to me.

But He was listening now. I wasn't asking Him for help or for my life, yet now He was present; I could feel His closeness as I prepared myself for the plunge under the ice.

Don't do it! came the feeling.

I was mystified. I had set my mind on the plan.

Don't do it! came the feeling again.

My mind told me one thing, but His presence told me another. I had to decide now, this second.

I gave myself over to that inner command. But then I had no hope.

It was a matter of minutes, maybe two, when I saw the police car on the yachting club island and nearby, across the stretch of obviously treacherous ice, I saw a policeman standing in the dusk, looking at me. "Throw me a rope!" I yelled. He disappeared. At first I had had a surge of optimism, but now that he was gone from me, I despaired. "Hurry," I said to myself frantically. "Hurry!" Could he know how little time I had left?

I heard voices. "We're going to throw you a rope."

Throw it now! I thought to myself. I could feel the paralysis setting in. It came fast. At first I couldn't move my legs. My arms stiffened. There was no part of me that I could move. No longer now was I thinking about ropes. I was thinking about . . . boyhood vacations on Mackinac Island . . . Sylva and me on a flying honeymoon . . . sailing on a moonlit night . . .

My hands . . . I saw my hands slip away from the surface of the ice. Yet I was experiencing a peace that was serene and actually pleasant. I felt my head go under the water. I felt icy water entering my mouth. I was sinking, but now I could move neither arms nor legs. I was rigid.

And then, suddenly, mysteriously, the power was there. I *could* move my arms. I pushed them down in the water. My head came up. I breathed again. And there in front of me was an orange life preserver. The last thing I remember was reaching for it.

o   o   o

My next awareness was opening my eyes and seeing the doctor peering into my face. He said, "There's someone here I'm sure you want to see." It was Sylva.

"How did I get here?" I asked, bewildered. Her answer was a litany of many miracles.

A bus was crossing the bridge at the precise moment I fell through the ice. The driver, sitting high up, saw me and radioed his dispatcher, who called the police. A girl happened to be walking along our river-front road on her way to a baby-sitting job. She heard my cries for help and rushed to our neighbor's house. The neighbor stepped outside, saw me in the river, and then she also called the police.

A policeman came, then went to his car to radio for extra help, while I held on to the orange life preserver that had been thrown to me. My rescuers were able to walk about halfway out on the ice before it started to crack, and a rope was thrown, which they say I grabbed, but let slip through my hands when they started to pull on it.

By then a crowd had gathered on the island. Three times my head went under the water, each time the crowd gasping, shouting that I was gone, and three times my head came back up, spouting water. Finally a dinghy was found and one of the policemen rushed it to the spot where I was appearing and disappearing. I was submerged, completely out of sight before he could get to me, but he reached his arm down over the dinghy into the water and, miraculously, connected with the collar of my jacket. The dinghy nearly capsized as he tried to drag me into it, but he hung on to me as I dangled from its side, and we were pulled to safety. Oxygen in the ambulance kept me alive during the rush to the hospital.

Later I figured that I was in the freezing water a minimum of twelve minutes. I was unconscious for three hours. The doctor in the emergency room at the hospital said he never saw a person alive with a pH blood factor as low as mine—six. When I was in the icy water I was not aware of the pain, but I was shivering from cold when I came to, calling for blankets. I spent one night in the intensive-care unit of the hospital and, to the doctors' amazement, the patient who was in critical condition on arrival was permitted to return home the next day. Two months later my heart was back to normal, and eight months later the nerves in my arms and legs had regenerated.

It took about a week for me to believe fully that I wasn't just dreaming and was really living. Since then, life for me has taken on a new meaning. I am more appreciative of being alive. I feel very grateful to God for sparing my life and to the five people who had a major part in my rescue. Since then, too, a lot of questions have been answered for me.

Where did the message come from that stopped me from my rash plan to swim under the ice?

When my body was paralyzed, where did the power come from that let my arms move again?

When I was unconscious under the water, why didn't the current sweep me downstream?

I know the answers to those questions now, for I've learned that God is always listening. He hears our prayers. When it is within His plan to answer them, He can work miracles. He did for me.

HE

Restores

HEALTH

*For I will restore health to you,
and your wounds I will heal,*

      says the Lord.
      —JEREMIAH 30:17, RSV

WHEN I AM SORE BESET
—*Antoinette Goetschius*

When I am sore beset, I seek some quiet place,
Some lonely room or barren windswept hill,
And there in silence wait apart until
I see again the smile upon God's face,
Until His presence floods me like the dawn,
And I can hear His whispered, "Peace be still,"
And know again the strength to do His will.
I turn to take my load and find it gone.

THE UNTOUCHABLE
Mark Miller

In June 1977, it seemed that everything was going my way. I'd graduated from college with honors, had married Shirley, a sweet, wonderful girl, and was working in my family's honey business in southern California. I was planning to start law school in September, and our first baby was due the same month. How excited I felt. How fulfilled!

But early one morning that summer a frightening change began to take place. I'd started out jogging my usual one-mile circuit, and about halfway through it, the strength suddenly went out of my body. I practically passed out. It was all I could do to stagger back to the house and collapse on the couch.

What could be happening to me? My arms and legs felt as if they were made of lead. I had no energy or vitality.

I went to a doctor who put me through a battery of tests. "It's perplexing," he told me. "Your tests show nothing abnormal." Doctor after doctor gave me the same answer.

Now, besides the extreme weakness and fatigue, I was gradually having nausea and other digestive troubles. I grew more and more nervous and couldn't sleep. I entered a Loma Linda, California, hospital for a thorough examination. Again, the doctors found no abnormal test results. Yet something was terribly wrong with me.

We went on searching for a diagnosis. Shirley and I had been taught to take our problems to the Lord, and we prayed for some kind of reassurance. But it seemed that God wasn't answering. The doctors continued to be baffled.

In September I struggled to start law school, but soon, when I couldn't even muster the energy to walk to classes, I knew I had to give up. When our son Adam was born, I stood over his crib and prayed, "Please, Father, bless me with the strength to be a good father to this special little boy." How I longed for strength and guidance from my Father in Heaven! I felt lost, alone.

By the first of the year, 1978, it was clear that my condition was still worse. Gradually I began to notice the effect that certain ordinary things in the house had on me, things like cold cream or strong cleaning agents. A whiff of Shirley's perfume would make me feel dizzy and nauseated. On the day that our lawn was treated with chemical weed killer and fertilizer, I literally thought I was dying. I felt so much inner tension, so much pressure inside of me, it seemed my body would burst. We had to flee the house.

We went to my sister's. But as luck would have it, some workmen came to tar her roof. The fresh tar brought the same misery as the weed killer. We went to another relative's house until a road was resurfaced in the neighborhood, forcing us to leave. These common types of chemical application were toxic to me for an incredibly long time. We were driven to move at least a dozen times—to the homes of other relatives, to motels and apartments—all in an effort to find a place where I could just be sick without being violently ill.

During this period, morning and night, month after month, we went on praying. Family members and friends prayed for us consistently. Still, with all this outpouring of faith, my health didn't improve. And the months went by.

In January 1979, Shirley read about a hospital in Dallas with an Environmental Control Unit specializing in problems like mine. In February I was admitted to this unit at Brookhaven Medical Center, in the care of Dr. William Rea. For nearly six weeks, I underwent tests, many of them "double blind"—

which means that neither the nurse nor I knew whether I was being exposed to a chemical substance or pure water.

After Dr. Rea had analyzed the test results, he came to me. "You've had a breakdown in your immune system," he explained. "It's called 'environmental disease,' and it means you can't tolerate modern chemicals—none of them. The only cure we know is to avoid chemicals as much as possible—and hope your immune system gets enough rest to rebuild itself."

Just what this avoidance meant was brought home to us when a nurse gave me my instructions. "Drink only bottled water. All your food should come from farms where pesticides and other chemicals aren't used. Wear all-cotton clothing. Get rid of any synthetic furnishings in your house, and stay clear of chemical cleansers, detergents, and perfumes." She gave me a detailed list of things to avoid and information on how to go about it. Dr. Rea wished me well and urged me to stay in touch by telephone.

From that day on, my wife, Shirley, our son, Adam, and I became fugitives from twentieth-century chemicals. Back in California we found a two-family house in Santa Barbara near the ocean and began to live our lives according to the instructions I'd been given at the hospital. My condition seemed to improve, but only for a while. Five months after we'd left Brookhaven, our landlord, who lived above us, told me that exterminators were coming to spray for fleas. We left the house before the spraying and returned several hours later. Even with these precautions, the fumes were intolerable to me. I hurried away, while Shirley packed our things.

Again, we were on the run, living with different family members throughout California, Arizona, and Utah, never able to stay long in any one place. Our second son, Jarom, was born in March 1980, but I was not free to enjoy him. By now I was sleeping in my car in the hills at night to avoid the chemicals used in neighborhoods and farming areas. I came home to my family just long enough to eat a couple of times a day. In between, sick and weak, I sometimes sat in the car in a parking lot, praying, reading my Bible, feeling a kinship with Jesus— especially when I read His words to the scribe: "Foxes have holes, and birds of the air have nests; but the Son of man has nowhere to lay his head" (Matthew 8:20).

Sometimes I wrote in the journal I'd been keeping all my

adult life. This is the entry for May 3, 1980: "How horrible I feel! The people across the street put chemical fertilizers on their lawn. I stayed too long, and now I'm very sick. I feel like everything is hopeless. I want to die. Why must I suffer on and on and on? I feel like every cell in my body is going to burst. God, help me, please."

I continued to live in my car until August, when we decided to try moving into my parents' home in the Los Angeles area again. We told our neighbors about my problem, and they gladly cooperated by not using outdoor chemicals. But the months of running had weakened me further, and my basic intolerance was worse, especially my skin sensitivity. I had to be extremely careful of everything I touched or wore, and where I sat or lay down. The house had to be off limits to outsiders because of the chemical residues they would bring in. Whenever members of my own family returned from work or shopping, they had to shower and change into clothes worn only at home. I could only bear having the television on for a brief time because the plastic components gave off fumes when they heated up. My reading was limited to books that were old and out of public circulation; otherwise ink fumes and chemical residues affected me.

Dr. Rea offered suggestions and encouragement over the phone as best he could. Meanwhile, I'd found a doctor in nearby Malibu, Dr. Edward Wagner, who understood my condition and who was a great comfort to me because he was a spiritual man. It was about this time that I started rereading the Book of Job in the Bible. I was fascinated by this ancient story of an upright man undergoing troubles and torment that he had done nothing to deserve, marveling at the parallels I found with my own condition. I saw Job afflicted and living in constant pain, but steadfastly refusing to turn his back on God.

I had thought of suicide. Job had wanted to die, too. But he never lost faith in God: "Though he slay me, yet will I trust in him," Job said resolutely (13:15).

When my own pain and despair threatened to overwhelm me, I clung to that. Could I be like Job? Could I keep my faith, no matter what?

When my twenty-seventh birthday came, there was no earthly possession I wanted—or could use. Instead of gifts, I asked for a day of fasting and prayer. We knelt in a circle as a family

and, one by one, prayed to our Heavenly Father. We thanked Him for the many things we had learned, and asked Him if He would please restore my health. We had a warm feeling in our hearts, knowing our prayers were heard. But in the days that followed, my skin became so sensitive that the slightest contact would burn like fire. Sometimes my reaction and tension were so severe that I'd gasp for breath, scream and cry, then fall to the rug, limp and exhausted.

It was so hard for my little boys to remember not to touch their daddy. One morning when I came out of my room while the rest of the family were having breakfast, Jarom tried to run to me.

"Daddy! Daddy!" he called, a delighted grin on his face, his arms reaching for me.

How I wanted to sweep him up in my arms, nuzzle his neck, and carry him for a piggyback ride around the table. But I had to turn away. It broke my heart.

Finally the day came when I asked Shirley to take the boys and move back to her parents' home in Utah. She had to do it, for the children's sakes as well as for my own physical health.

Saying good-bye, we cried. We knew we couldn't be together again as a family until my health improved. And I had never been worse!

Once more I went back to the Bible, back to the words of Job: "My lyre is turned to mourning, and my pipe to the voice of those who weep" (30:31, RSV). "Yes," I said out loud, "Job felt as I feel." Then I read on: "With God are wisdom and might; he has counsel and understanding" (12:13, RSV) and "When he has tried me, I shall come forth as gold" (23:10, RSV). "Yes," I said, "I must believe that. I must. I must."

My immunity weakened to the point where I had to stay in one room, isolated from everyone, never venturing into the rest of the house. I talked to my mother on the intercom. She cooked my meals and left my food on a tray outside the door. If she so much as picked up the tray after using a detergent on her hands, I would get a severe reaction if I touched that spot on the tray. My only contact with the outside world was the telephone, but even holding the plastic receiver too long could make me dizzy and anxious. I was a prisoner, an untouchable. I was desperately alone.

Then, during this time of extreme loneliness and despair, an answer came to our four years of praying. I began to feel a deep peace within me, a peace I had *never* felt before. I heard no voices. I saw no angels. Yet I had a powerful conviction in my heart and mind. Something in me seemed to say the words, *You will be well very, very soon.*

I did not seem to improve, but the warmth and peace I felt lasted for four weeks, during June and July 1981.

Then, on the morning of July 20, I was aware of a sense of deep sorrow. I felt hopeless against some dark power greater than my own. But, just as I thought I'd be completely overcome with loneliness and sadness, it happened. I felt myself lifted on eagles' wings; I seemed to soar beyond the fog and clouds into the clear blue sky. A warmth suffused my whole body, a healing warmth. The invisible bars fell away. I felt suddenly, totally, confidently free. Free! With a new strength pouring into me, I went to the bedroom door. Quietly I pushed it open, knowing absolutely that I no longer needed to fear the outside world. My eyes filled with tears. I found my mother and hugged her.

"Mark!" she whispered. "What's happened?"

"I'm well," I said firmly. "I've been healed." I *knew* it was so.

I couldn't wait to get back to Shirley and the children. I got in our car only to find it wouldn't start. I tried to prime it by putting gasoline in the carburetor, and I spilled some all over my hand. But there was no toxic reaction. Nothing. "O God, thank You. Thank You."

Within forty-eight hours I was on my way to Utah and my family. Wanting to surprise them, I waited until I was a short distance away and then telephoned.

"Hi, Shirley."

"Hello, sweetheart. How are you feeling today?"

"I'm better."

"I'm glad you're having a better day today."

"No, I'm well. I'm healed. I'm in Fillmore, and I'll be there soon to bring you home."

Shirley could hardly find words. "Should we change our clothes?" she finally asked. "Should we fix a special room for you?"

"All of that's behind us. The Lord has made me well."

When I drove up to the house, Shirley, Adam, and Jarom were waiting on the steps for me. No words can express the joy I felt as I wrapped my arms around them. God had truly wrought a glorious miracle in our lives. Later I went to Dallas and Dr. Rea examined me. He was thrilled by my unusual recovery. "You're totally tolerant and totally well," he told me.

Currently, I'm working in the family honey business, operating a honey store in the mountain apple-orchard community of Oak Glen, California. At church I enjoy teaching a Sunday school class.

At home, I love being a normal husband and daddy. My little boys can run to me whenever they want. And Shirley says, "I know how Lazarus' family must have felt when he walked out of the tomb."

I am alive again after four years of a living death. I give all the credit to our Father in Heaven, who loves us and hears us. I have learned that no matter how much we may have to suffer, we never have more than we can bear. I have learned that if you hang on to your faith, as Job did, God answers your prayers in His own perfect way.

THE MESSAGE
Ginger Davis Gettle

"I'm going to die, aren't I?" I said to my husband. "Tell me!"

Bob pulled his chair close to my hospital bed and took my hand. "You have to have another operation," he said, "maybe two. The tests taken after your stroke show you have two weak spots in the arteries in your brain. If they're not repaired, you'll have another stroke." He didn't add, ". . .and *that* stroke will be fatal," but I knew that's what he meant.

I pulled my hand away. "How much will it cost?"

His voice sank to a whisper. "About two hundred and fifty thousand dollars," he said, ". . . or more."

I closed my eyes and sank back against my pillow. Two hundred and fifty thousand dollars—when we barely had enough to pay the grocery bills. And even if we had the money, I was so traumatized by just the thought of surgery that I couldn't imagine going through it. Plus I had a history of health problems—ulcers, allergic reactions, unusual complications after other medical procedures—that didn't bode well for *any* operation, much less highly complicated ones.

"What happens if I don't have the surgery, Bob?" I asked. "I'll die, won't I?"

Bob didn't answer. Instead he moved onto the edge of my bed and put his arms around me. But I barely felt them. *This is it,* I thought. *The end of my life.* And the end of a year filled with one devastating event after another.

The past year in Houston had been terrible for us. Oil prices had plunged and Bob had been laid off from his job on an offshore oil rig. He'd been looking for work steadily, but nothing had come up. In the meantime his unemployment checks had stopped and our savings had dwindled away.

Next came the news that Bob's mother had Alzheimer's disease and his father had a malignant tumor. Bob and I moved in with Mom and Pop to care for them. Foolish as it was, we put off getting health insurance; we didn't have a cent to spare, and Bob would be getting a job any day now. Or so we thought.

I too was in a downward spiral of sinking spirits and increasing health problems. And then this! When I awoke one morning in late November my right leg and arm were strangely "asleep," and my mouth couldn't form the words I wanted to say. I managed to throw myself out of bed and into the hall, but then I collapsed. I was rushed to the hospital.

For two weeks I couldn't talk or communicate. I had never been so frightened. I went through a series of exhausting tests—and now Bob was at my side telling me the results:

Without the money, no operation.

Without the operation, no life.

"Then I'll just die," I said.

His arms tightened around me. But I pulled away. As much as I loved him, I wanted him to leave. "Go home," I said. "You need the rest." Inside of me the message was different: *I'm going to die. Go away. Leave me alone.*

Slowly he pulled on his jacket. After he left, the room was silent. *Thank goodness the other bed is empty,* I thought. I couldn't stand to have anybody else near me.

There was the squish of rubber-soled shoes in the corridor. I turned my head to see a wheelchair roll in, pushed by a smiling nurse. "Good news, Mrs. Gettle. You're getting company," she said.

A roommate! That was all I needed. I watched grudgingly as a slender black woman was helped out of the chair and into the adjoining bed. She had a pleasant face framed by soft gray hair. "Hello," she said, looking over as the nurse adjusted her covers. "I'm Flossie."

"Hello," I said wearily.

"What are you here for?" Flossie's voice was warm and friendly, but I was in no mood for talking. Tersely I explained my physical condition.

"When are they going to fix you up?" Flossie asked.

Never, I thought to myself, choking back tears. "There are some problems," I said. "We can't afford the surgery." As the nurse turned to go, I asked her to pull the curtains around my bed. "I'd like some privacy," I said weakly.

The curtains rattled on their rod, then closed around me like a tent, and Flossie vanished out of sight behind them. Vaguely I heard some muffled conversation about a mysterious attack that Flossie had had that evening. Her husband had rushed her to the hospital, and she was being kept overnight for observation.

But I paid little attention to what was going on. I curled up in misery.

I'd always been a "Christian" person. My mother had been a minister, and I had gone through all the right motions and participated in all the right church activities. But what good had it all done?

I felt totally abandoned. How would my husband cope when I was gone? Who would take care of Mom and Pop? Fears swirled in terrifying profusion.

The words sounded in my mind, with every breath I took. *You'll die, you'll die, you'll die* . . .

I fell into a heavy, churning sleep . . .

"Mrs. Gettle, wake up!" A voice called me; a hand was shaking my shoulder gently but firmly. The curtains that shrouded my bed had parted; a form leaned over me, silhouetted against the eerie glow of a small night-light in the corridor outside.

"What's wrong?" I mumbled.

"Nothing's wrong, honey," said a rich, gentle voice. "I have a message for you. From God."

From God? Flossie?

It *was* Flossie. She had left her own bed and was standing next to mine.

"I've been praying about you," she said, "and God spoke to me clear as a bell. He said, " 'Tell this lady I'm going to give her her surgery, and it's going to be successful.' " She patted my hand. "Now don't you worry about another thing. You'll *live.*"

With a tremble of the curtains, she was gone. I lay staring at the glowing hall light. The small clock on my bedside table said it was 2:30 in the morning, the middle of the night.

Abruptly I was filled with an overwhelming sense of peace. It was as if gentle hands had grasped my shoulders and turned me completely around. The hammering, negative voice in my head stopped. It was replaced with a fresher, calmer cadence. *You'll live, you'll live, you'll live . . .* I drifted back to sleep and slept better than I had in months.

The next morning I was released from the hospital. I was told that, short of having the necessary surgery, nothing further could be done for me. As I packed my things to go home, Flossie smiled knowingly from the next bed. "It will be all right, honey," she said with such conviction that it was impossible to doubt her. "God told me so."

Bob looked at me strangely as he drove me home. "It's good to see you so cheerful," he said. "Especially since you don't feel well."

Don't feel well? After months of illness and depression, I was feeling better and better. Instead of slumping down onto my bed the way I might have a few days before, I had the urge to get busy in the house, maybe even to check in with the neighbors to see what had happened since I'd been away.

You'll live. God will give you your surgery.

I saw my neighbor's car pass the window and pull into the driveway next door.

My neighbor, Dr. Howard Derman—I'd said hello to him over the fence, but that was all. But suddenly it hit me that he was a neurologist. He'd know more about what they told me in the hospital. I was out the door before my astonished husband could ask where I was going.

Dr. Derman was at his kitchen table having breakfast. I told him about my diagnosis and asked him to explain.

He drew on his napkin to illustrate. "There are two weak places in your arteries that bulge out," he explained. "If they aren't repaired, they can blow out, just like a weak spot on a tire." He went into more detail about the surgery, then asked who would be doing it.

"No one," I said. "We can't afford it."

He looked thoughtful for a moment, then began asking questions about Bob and me and our finances. "I'm affiliated with a local hospital," he said. On a previous visit there I'd been told I wasn't "destitute enough" to qualify for special assistance.

"It just seems to me," he went on, "that if ever two people needed special funding, it's you and Bob. Let me see what I can do."

It's hard to believe what happened next. Since my case was so unusual, the doctors asked if my operation could be filmed for teaching and research purposes, and the hospital would pay all charges. Is that what Flossie's incredible statement meant: "Tell this lady I'm going to *give* her her surgery"?

Bob couldn't get over how calm I was as they rolled me down toward the operating room, clutching a piece of paper bearing the words, *Let not your heart be troubled* (John 14:1).

I went through nearly nine hours of complicated surgery to repair the first aneurysm—and it all went smoothly. Within a few days I was up and walking in the halls. The doctors were amazed at my quick recovery. Ordinarily they would have sent me home for a few months to recover and regain my strength for the second operation, but I felt so strong and confident that I said, "Let's go ahead now."

Only thirteen days later I had another operation—and four days after that I was out of intensive care and walking around the wards, helping the nurses with some of their duties. No more lying around thinking about dying for me! The hospital staff could hardly believe it. When they commented on how well I was coping, I gave the explanation I'd given from the first.

"Oh," they said, laughing, "you're back to 'God gave me the surgery,' are you?" But I could tell they were impressed.

What turned me around—from a timid, fear-filled person to a confident, lively one? A lot of people would say it was the power of suggestion and I agree: God's suggestion, passed on by one of His faithful messengers and given to a desperate woman deep in despair in the middle of the night. How did that messenger happen to be in the bed next to mine that fateful night? That's one of the mysteries, for the doctors never found anything wrong with Flossie. She went home fine, and has stayed fine. I know, because Flossie and I have been fast friends ever since.

"When I woke you up that night," Flossie once said, "you must have wondered, 'What on earth's got into her?'"

And then she and I laughed, because we knew. It was nothing on earth.

Nothing on earth at all.

 ## THE LONGEST WAIT OF MY LIFE
Mary Ann Fenyus

How well I remember the terrifying sense of aloneness that swept through me the day I knew for sure that I was going blind.

Not that I was surprised. I'd worn those awful thick glasses since I was twelve, and by themselves they caused me to feel isolated. No one wanted to play with the thin girl whose eyes were made beady by bottle-glass lenses.

But it wasn't until the spring of 1963, when I was twenty-nine years old and a teaching nun with the Sisters of St. Joseph, that the real blow fell. One morning I stood before my fifty wiggly first graders in St. Bernard's Parochial School just outside of Pittsburgh. The children were working on their A-B-Cs. I had made seven-inch-high paper cutout letters, pasted them on white showcards, and propped them up around the room. Big as the cutouts were, they were unrecognizable to me unless

I stood right next to them. So I memorized where key letters were. ABC in back of me. GHI to my right. MNO in front of me across the classroom.

On this morning one of the children in the back of the room missed a letter.

"Try again, Amy," I said.

The whole class started to titter. "I'm not *Amy,* Sister," a voice was saying from the blurred distance. "I'm *Bob!*"

Panic. I could no longer hide how bad my vision had become. That very day I started a round of visits to my superiors, desperately trying to see what could be done. The mother general sent me to see her own specialist, Dr. Jay Linn, Jr., of Pittsburgh. I was sitting now on the swivel stool in Dr. Linn's office, nervously fingering the sleeves of my black habit as he pulled back the slit lamp through which he had been examining the insides of my eyes.

"Yes, it is keratoconus, Sister," said Dr. Linn. "The cornea of your eye makes a cone instead of being rounded."

I tried to make Dr. Linn's face come into focus. "How bad is it, then?" My voice was barely audible.

"A few years ago you'd have gone blind. First your left eye; eventually your right." But then for the first time one word was spoken that gave me hope. *Transplant.* Today, Dr. Linn was saying, we can lift out the healthy cornea of a donor who has just died (age makes little difference) and insert it in the eye of a recipient.

"The key," Dr. Linn said, "is to find corneas. We have eye banks, but the term is misleading because there is no real bank of eyes you can draw on." A cornea apparently will perish in just a few hours, so surgeons constantly need new ones, and not enough people are making eye donations. "We have a long waiting list, Sister. But there's always a chance."

I signed up that very day and when I got back to the convent I packed a hospital bag with an extra nightgown, my bedcap, toothbrush, missal, and rosary. But a month went by. Two. Three. Four months passed. Vacation time came, and in June I moved to our Mother House in Baden, Pennsylvania, where the wait went on into mid-July. I would jump whenever a phone rang somewhere in the convent. But it was like my childhood all over again: the calls were never for me.

Meanwhile my eyes were getting progressively worse. Behind those ugly prism glasses I could hardly see out of my left eye, and my right wasn't much better. Heavy lines appeared beneath words when I tried to read. Then moved up *into* the words, making them almost impossible to interpret.

I was praying constantly during my long wait. So was my family in Beaver, Pennsylvania. So were the nuns who knew my situation. But unknown to me, another kind of prayer was being brought to bear — not one of words, but of deeds.

One day a few months earlier, on Easter Sunday, the assistant pastor at the Westminster Presbyterian Church in nearby Upper St. Clair Township told his congregation about the outcome of his own recent operation. He had regained his failing sight through corneal transplants. He urged his congregation to pledge eye donations to the local eye bank. One of the families who responded was the Gillilands, Will, June, and their five children, including a daughter named Julie, the second oldest, twelve years old. I had no idea of their existence then.

Now it was the night of July 17. Even though it was only nine o'clock, I was in my cell preparing for bed. We had to be up at 5:20 for Matins and Lauds, so it was lights out at ten, but there was no point in trying to read until then because the words on the page were all smudged now. I knelt on the hardwood floor in my white nightgown and white bedcap beside the brown bed in that little nine-by-twelve room, looking up at my crucifix. I prayed for a while, then turned back the sheet and crawled in.

Suddenly I had an intense feeling that someone was in danger. I sat upright. Had I been asleep — had a bad dream? What time was it? I turned on the light and struggled hard to read the clock on my nightstand. It was only 9:30.

At that moment my thin body gave a shudder. "Father, I'm just realizing! Before I can see again, someone has to die." But of course — that's why corneal recipients rarely knew who their donors were. The knowledge was too much to bear. I shuddered again. Out loud I quoted from the Requiem Mass. "Father," I said, "grant unto them eternal rest."

But why had I said *them*?

I lay in my narrow bed praying for unknown people in an

unknown situation. Yet, mysteriously, I was aware of my *connectedness* with them. I, who had been so alone, was in profound communion with people I would doubtless never meet. When I went to sleep I was still praying for them.

The convent's bells rang. Morning. I groped my way to chapel for Matins and Lauds. And all the while I went on praying, interceding for . . . for whom? For what?

A few hours later I heard a phone ring. Shortly the assistant mother general came running down the hall.

"The call's come through, Sister! They want you right away."

I didn't wait for the elevator. As fast as I dared, I made my way upstairs, grabbed my overnight bag, and within an hour was being admitted to the Pittsburgh Eye and Ear Hospital.

Dr. Linn told me he could let me have one cornea and would operate on my left eye. He bandaged my somewhat stronger right eye, then numbed my left with a local anesthetic, his soothing voice talking me through everything that was happening. About three hours into the operation, searing light smashed into my left eye. The new cornea was in place. I could see!

The ceiling. The operating-room lights. The outline of a nurse on my left side. Dr. Linn's hand near my face.

Everything was going perfectly, and yet, as I was returned to my hospital room, both eyes still bandaged, I continued to marvel at the experience I'd had a few hours earlier of "knowing" that someone was in danger.

My parents arrived as soon as I could have visitors. From behind my bandages I heard my mother's excited voice. "So, it's the best news! You are going to see!" We spent a happy time talking about the gift of sight. Then, pausing as if making a decision, Mother said, "I know who gave you her cornea."

"But that's not possible, Mother. The donor's name is a secret."

I heard the rattling of a newspaper. "There was a dreadful car accident last night. Half a family was killed: the father, his fifteen-year-old son and twelve-year-old daughter. When I was waiting for the elevator just now I heard hospital people talking. Your cornea belongs to the little girl. Her name is Julie."

As soon as I could, I wrote to the mother, June Gilliland. It was a confusing letter to write and I half expected Mrs. Gilliland never to answer. After all . . .

But by return mail came a letter, one that I could *read!*
Would I come to Upper St. Clair Township?

Which of course I did. I met June and her three small
daughters, each wearing her hair in long bangs. I found that I
was not at all shy. I seemed to know just what to say and soon
was urging June to talk about the night of the accident.

After a family picnic celebrating her husband's thirty-ninth
birthday, the Gillilands had returned home in two cars. Will
and all five of the children were in one automobile, while June
took her own mother home by another route. Will Gilliland—
a safety engineer by profession, a sensible man by nature—
always drove with care. The police pieced together the details.
A gray car, without lights, sped out of the night straight at
Will in Will's lane. The seventy-year-old driver of the other car
was drunk.

June for her part seemed to know just what to say to me too,
almost as if she were living inside my confusion. June told me
about Julie. I held her picture in my hand. Dark-haired. A good
student. Outgoing. Julie was twelve years old when she died,
the very age when I had last seen my childhood world clearly. I
spoke of my sense of guilt at knowing someone had to die before
I could see. Again, June knew just what to say. She took the
picture of Julie from my hands and spoke words that healed.
"Never forget," she said, looking at her child, "death is inevita-
ble, love is not."

Yes, that was true. In donating her eyes, Julie had chosen a
path of involvement. As June and I talked I glimpsed the hope
that my eyesight was just one part of a larger healing taking
place. I could see my physical world more clearly now, but there
was also a new insight into the world of the Spirit where my
tragedy is connected to others, my joy is others' too. In that
realm death and life touch each other.

Strange. Had I once before been to this universe, where all of us
are again connected, as perhaps we were in the beginning? I
remembered the night in my cell, the night of the accident. Into
my mind sprang the memory of sitting upright in bed, aware of
danger, struggling to read the face of the clock beside my bed.

"June . . ." I said, almost afraid to ask. "That night . . . did
the police fix the *time* of the accident?"

"Yes," June said. "We do know. It was 9:30."

THE HEALING OF MAUDE BLANFORD
Catherine Marshall

Healing through faith remains a mystery to me. I have been part of prayer campaigns where it was gloriously granted, others where, at least in this world, it was not.

Why? There are no glib answers. Yet in my experience, as God has closed one door, He always opens another.

Last summer, a new friend from Louisville, Kentucky, opened a door on this difficult question by telling me of Maude Blanford's healing from terminal cancer eleven years ago. I was so intrigued that I flew to Louisville and got the details from Maude herself.

The woman across the dining table from me was a grand-motherly type, comfortable to be with. "How did your—ah, illness begin?" I asked, feeling foolish even asking the question to someone obviously in such radiant health.

"My left leg had been hurting me," Mrs. Blanford replied. "I thought it was because I was on my feet so much. Finally my husband and I decided that I should go to the doctor."

When her family doctor said words like "specialist" and "biopsy," the patient read the unspoken thought—malignancy.

Mrs. Blanford was referred to Dr. O. J. Hayes. He examined her on June 29, 1959, and prescribed radiation treatment. The treatment began July 7, and was followed by surgery on September 29. After the operation, when Mrs. Blanford pleaded with Doctor Hayes for the truth, he admitted, "It *is* cancer and it's gone too far. We could not remove it because it's so widespread. One kidney is almost nonfunctioning. The pelvic bone is affected—that's why you have the pain in your leg."

Maude Blanford was put on narcotics to control the by now excruciating pain and sent home to die. Over a six-month period, while consuming a thousand dollars' worth of pain-relieving drugs, she took stock of her spiritual resources and found them meager indeed. There was no church affiliation, no knowledge of the Bible, only the most shadowy concept of Jesus.

In January 1960, she suffered a cerebral hemorrhage and was rushed back to the hospital. For twelve days she lay unconscious. But Maude Blanford, oblivious to the world around her, was awake in a very different world. In her deep coma, a vivid image came to her. She saw a house with no top on it. The partitions between the rooms were there, the furniture in place, but there was no roof. She remembered thinking, *Oh, we must put a roof on it!*

When she came out of the coma, Mrs. Blanford's mind was very much intact, but bewildered. What could the roofless house have meant? As she puzzled over it, a Presence seemed to answer her. Today she has no hesitation in calling Him the Holy Spirit. "He seemed to show me that the house represented my body, but that without Jesus as my covering, my body had no protection."

From then until July 1960, her condition worsened. Heart action and breathing became so difficult, she was reduced to weak whispers. Even with drugs, the suffering became unbearable.

By July she knew she no longer had the strength to make the trip for radiation treatment. "On July first I told the nurse I wouldn't be coming back."

But that day, as her son-in-law helped her into the car outside the medical building, she broke down and wept. "At that moment I didn't want anything except for God to take me quickly—as I was. I said, 'God, I don't know who You are. I don't know anything about You. I don't even know how to pray. Just, Lord, have Your own way with me.' "

Though she did not realize it, Maude Blanford had just prayed one of the most powerful of all prayers—the prayer of relinquishment. By getting her own mind and will out of the way, she had opened the door to the Holy Spirit.

She did not have long to wait for evidence of His presence. Monday, July 4, dawned beautiful but hot. That afternoon Joe Blanford set up a cot for his wife outdoors under the trees. As the ill woman rested, into her mind poured some beautiful sentences.

"Is not this the fast that I have chosen? to loose the bands of wickedness, to undo the heavy burdens, and to let the oppressed go free . . .? Then shall thy light break forth . . . speedily. . . . Here I am."

I stared at Maude Blanford over the rim of my coffee cup. "But I thought you didn't know the Bible."

"I didn't! I'd never read a word of it. Only I knew this didn't sound like ordinary English. I thought, *Is that in the Bible?* And right away the words came: *Isaiah 58.* Well, my husband got a Bible for me. I had to hunt and hunt to find the part called Isaiah. But then when I found those verses just exactly as I had heard them—except for the last three words, 'Here I am'— well, I knew God Himself had really spoken to me!"

Over the next weeks Maude Blanford read the Bible constant- ly, often until two or three o'clock in the morning, seeing the Person of Jesus take shape before her eyes. As she read, a response grew in her, a response that is another of the Holy Spirit's workings in the human heart—praise. At home she began very slowly climbing the stairs, praising Jesus for each step she attained.

Next she tried putting a small amount of water in a pail. Sitting in a kitchen chair, she would mop the floor in the area immediately around her, scoot the chair a few inches, mop again. "Thank You, Jesus, for helping me do this!"

Her daughter-in-law, who was coming over almost daily to clean house for her, one day asked in great puzzlement, "Mom, how is it that your kitchen floor never gets dirty?"

The older woman smiled. "Well, I guess I'll have to confess—the Lord and I are doing some housework."

But their chief work, she knew, was not on this building of brick and wood, but on the house of her spirit, the house that had been roofless for so long. Gradually, as her knowledge of Him grew, she sensed His protective love surrounding and sheltering her. Not that all pain and difficulties were over. She was still on pain-numbing narcotics, still experiencing much nausea from the radiation.

One Saturday night, when the pain would not let her sleep, she lay on her bed praising God and reading the Bible. About 2:00 A.M., she drifted off to sleep with the Bible lying on her stomach. She felt that she was being carried to Heaven, travel- ing a long way through space. Then came a Voice out of the universe, "My child, your work is not finished. You are to go back." This was repeated three times, slowly, majestically.

The rest of the night she remained awake, flooded with joy, thanking God. When her husband woke up in the morning, she told him, "Honey, Jesus healed me last night."

She could see that he did not believe it; there was no change in her outward appearance. "But I knew I was healed and that I had to tell people." That very morning she walked to the Baptist church across the highway from their home and asked the minister if she could give a testimony. He gave permission, and she told the roomful of people that God had spoken to her in the night and healed her.

A few weeks later she insisted on taking a long bus trip to visit her son in West Virginia. Still on narcotics, still suffering pain, she nonetheless knew that the Holy Spirit was telling her to rely from now on on Jesus instead of drugs. At five o'clock on the afternoon of April 27, 1961, on the return bus journey, as she popped a pain-killing pill into her mouth at a rest stop, she knew it would be the last one.

So it turned out. In retrospect, physicians now consider this sudden withdrawal as great a miracle as the transformation of cancer cells to healthy tissue.

It took time to rebuild her body-house—nine months for her bad leg to be near normal, two years for all symptoms of cancer to vanish. When she called Doctor Hayes in 1962 over some small matter he almost shouted in astonishment. "Mrs. Blanford! What's happened to you! I thought you were—"

"You thought I was long since gone," she said, laughing.

"Please come to my office at once and let me examine you! I've got to know what's happened."

"But why should I spend a lot of money for an examination when I'm a perfectly well woman?" she asked.

"Mrs. Blanford, I promise you, this one is on us!" What the doctor found can best be stated in his own words: "I had lost contact with Mrs. Blanford and had assumed that this patient had expired. In May of 1962 she appeared in my office. It had been two-and-a-half years since her operation and her last X ray had been in July 1960 . . . . The swelling of her leg was gone. She had full use of her leg; she had no symptoms whatsoever, and on examination I was unable to ascertain whether or not any cancer was left . . . .

"She was seen again on November 5, 1962, at which time her examination was completely negative . . . . She has been seen periodically since that time for routine examinations . . . . She is absolutely asymptomatic . . . . This case is most unusual in

that this woman had a proven, far-advanced metastatic cancer of
the cervix and there should have been no hope whatsoever for
her survival."

No hope whatsoever . . . No hope except the hope on which
our faith is founded.

The miracle of Maude Blanford reminds me again of that
scene on the night before His crucifixion when Jesus spoke
quietly to His despairing disciples, "Ye have not chosen me,
but I have chosen you" (John 15:16). He is still saying that to
us today, while His Spirit—always working through human
beings—sometimes confounds us, often amazes us, and is always the Guide to the future who can bring us joy and excited
fulfillment.

HE

Removes

THE STING OF DEATH

When the perishable puts on the imperishable, and the mortal puts on immortality, then shall come to pass the saying that is written:
   "Death is swallowed up in victory."
   "O death, where is thy victory?
   O death, where is thy sting?"
   . . . Thanks be to God, who gives us the victory through our Lord Jesus Christ.
               —1 CORINTHIANS 15:54–57, RSV

MISSING
—Author Unknown

When the anxious hearts say "Where?"
He doth answer "In My care."

"Is it life or is it death?"
"Wait," He whispers. "Child, have faith!"

"Were they frightened at the last?"
"No, the sting of death is past."

"Did a thought of 'Home-Love' rise?"
"I looked down through Mother-eyes."

"Saviour, tell us, where are they?"
"In My keeping, night and day."

"Tell us, tell us, how it stands."
"None shall pluck them from My Hands."

RETURN FROM TOMORROW
Dr. George C. Ritchie, Jr.

When I was sent to the base hospital at Camp Barkeley, Texas, early in December 1943, I had no idea I was seriously ill. I'd just completed basic training, and my only thought was to get on the train to Richmond, Virginia, to enter medical school as part of the army's doctor-training program. It was an unheard-of break for a private, and I wasn't going to let a chest cold cheat me out of it.

But days passed and I didn't get better. It was December 19 before I was moved to the recuperation wing, where a jeep was to pick me up at 4:00 A.M. the following morning to drive me to the railroad station.

A few more hours and I'd make it! Then about 9:00 P.M. I began to run a fever. I went to the ward boy and begged some aspirin.

Despite the aspirin, my head throbbed, and I'd cough into the pillow to smother the sounds. At 3:00 A.M. I decided to get up and dress.

The next half-hour is a blur for me. I remember being too weak to finish dressing. I remember a nurse coming to the room, and then a doctor, and then a bell-clanging ambulance ride to the X ray building. Could I stand, the captain was asking, long enough to get one picture? I struggled unsteadily to my feet.

The whir of the machine is the last thing I remember.

When I opened my eyes, I was lying in a little room I had never seen before. A tiny light burned in a nearby lamp. For a while I lay there, trying to recall where I was. All of a sudden I sat bolt upright. The train! I'd miss the train!

Now, I know that what I am about to describe will sound incredible. I do not understand it any more than I ask you to; all that I can do is relate the events of that night as they occurred. I sprang out of bed and looked around the room for my uniform. Not on the bedrail: I stopped, staring. Someone was lying in the bed I had just left.

I stepped closer in the dim light, then drew back. He was dead. The slack jaw, the gray skin were awful. Then I saw the ring. On his left hand was the Phi Gamma Delta fraternity ring I had worn for two years.

I ran into the hall, eager to escape the mystery of that room. Richmond, that was the all-important thing—getting to Richmond. I started down the hall for the outside door.

"Look out!" I shouted to an orderly bearing down on me. He seemed not to hear, and a second later he had passed the very spot where I stood as though I had not been there.

It was too strange to think about. I reached the door, went through, and found myself in the darkness outside, speeding toward Richmond. Running? Flying? I only know that the dark earth was slipping past while other thoughts occupied my mind, terrifying and unaccountable ones. The orderly had not seen me. What if the people at medical school could not see me either?

In utter confusion I stopped by a telephone pole in a town by a large river and put my hand against the guy wire. At least the wire *seemed* to be there, but my hand could not make contact with it. One thing was clear: in some unimaginable way I had lost my firmness of flesh, the hand that could grip that wire, the body that other people saw.

I was beginning to know too that the body on that bed was mine, unaccountably separated from me, and that my job was to get back and rejoin it as fast as I could.

Finding the base and the hospital again was no problem. Indeed, I seemed to be back there almost as soon as I thought of it. But where was the little room I had left? So began what must have been one of the strangest searches ever to take place: the search for myself. As I ran from one ward to the next, past room after room of sleeping soldiers, all about my age, I realized how unfamiliar we are with our own faces. Several times I stopped by a sleeping figure that was exactly as I imagined myself. But the fraternity ring, the Phi Gam ring, was lacking, and I would speed on.

At last I entered a little room with a single dim light. A sheet had been drawn over the figure on the bed, but the arms lay along the blanket. On the left hand was the ring.

I tried to draw back the sheet, but I could not seize it. And now that I had found myself, how could one join two people who were so completely separate? And there, standing before this problem, I thought suddenly: *This is death. This is what we human beings call "death," this splitting up of one's self.* It was the first time I had connected death with what had happened to me.

In that most despairing moment, the little room began to fill with light. I say "light," but there is no word in our language to describe brilliance that intense. I must try to find words, however, because incomprehensible as the experience was to my intellect, it has affected every moment of my life since then.

The light which entered that room was Christ. I knew because a thought was put deep within me: *You are in the presence of the Son of God.* I have called Him "light," but I could also have said "love," for that room was flooded, pierced, illuminated, by total compassion. It was a presence so comforting, so joyous and all-satisfying, that I wanted to lose myself forever in the wonder of it.

But something else was present in that room. With the presence of Christ (simultaneously, though I must tell it one by one), there also had entered every single episode of my entire life. There they were, every event and thought and conversation, as palpable as a series of pictures. There was no first or last, each one was contemporary, each one asked a single question, *What did you do with your time on earth?*

I looked anxiously among the scenes before me: school, home, scouting, and the cross-country track team—a fairly typical boyhood, yet in the light of that presence it seemed a trivial and irrelevant existence.

I searched my mind for good deeds.

Did you tell anyone about Me? came the question.

I didn't have time to do much, I answered. *I was planning to, then this happened. I'm too young to die!*

No one, the thought was inexpressibly gentle, *is too young to die.*

And now a new wave of light spread through the room, already so incredibly bright, and suddenly we were in another world. Or rather, I suddenly perceived all around us a very different world occupying the same space. I followed Christ through ordinary streets and countrysides, and everywhere I saw this other existence strangely superimposed on our familiar world.

It was thronged with people. People with the unhappiest faces I ever have seen. Each grief seemed different. I saw businessmen walking the corridors of the places where they had worked, trying vainly to get someone to listen to them. I saw a mother following a sixty-year-old man, her son I guessed, cautioning him, instructing him. He did not seem to be listening.

Suddenly I was remembering myself, that very night, caring about nothing but getting to Richmond. Was it the same for these people; had their hearts and minds been all concerned with earthly things, and now, having lost earth, were they still fixed hopelessly here? I wondered if this was hell: to care most when you are most powerless.

I was permitted to look at two more worlds that night—I cannot say "spirit worlds" for they were too real, too solid. Both were introduced the same way: a new quality of light, a new openness of vision, and suddenly it was apparent what had been there all along. The second world, like the first, occupied this very surface of the earth, but it was a vastly different realm. Here was no absorption with earthly things, but—for want of a better word—with truth.

I saw sculptors and philosophers here, composers and inventors. There were universities and great libraries and scientific laboratories that surpass the wildest inventions of science fiction.

Of the final world I had only a glimpse. Now we no longer seemed to be on earth, but immensely far away, out of all relation to it. And there, still at a great distance, I saw a city— but a city, if such a thing is conceivable, constructed out of light. At that time I had not read the Book of Revelation, nor, incidentally, anything on the subject of life after death. But here was a city in which the walls, houses, streets seemed to give off light, while moving among them were beings as blindingly bright as the One who stood beside me. This was only a moment's vision, for the next instant the walls of the little room closed around me, the dazzling light faded, and a strange sleep stole over me . . .

To this day, I cannot fully fathom why I was chosen to return to life. All I know is that when I woke up in the hospital bed in that little room, in the familiar world where I'd spent all my life, it was not a homecoming. The cry in my heart that moment has been the cry of my life since: Christ, show me Yourself again.

It was weeks before I was well enough to leave the hospital, and all that time one thought obsessed me: to get a look at my chart. At last I was left unattended; there it was in terse medical shorthand: Pvt. George Ritchie, died December 20, 1943, double lobar pneumonia.

Later I talked to the doctor who had signed the report. He told me there was no doubt in his mind that I was dead when he examined me, but nine minutes later the soldier who had been assigned to prepare me for the morgue came running to him to ask him to give me a shot of adrenalin. The doctor gave me a hypo of adrenalin directly into the heart muscle, all the while disbelieving what his own eyes were seeing. My return to life, he told me, without brain damage or other lasting effect, was the most baffling circumstance of his career.

Today I feel that I know why I had the chance to return to this life. It was to become a physician so that I could learn about man and then serve God. And every time I have been able to serve our God by helping some brokenhearted adult, treating some injured child, or counseling some teenager, then deep within I have felt that He was there beside me again.

RECITAL FOR ONE
Phyllis M. Letellier

My husband and I had been farming just a few years up to the summer our sons were two and four years old. We were trying hard to get established, so my husband still worked full time off the farm. My days were full—driving a tractor to do field work, tending livestock, trying to be a good homemaker and mother. But at one point there came a welcome lull in my labors. A good chance to get away.

I loaded the boys in our ten-year-old car and drove all the way across Wyoming to visit my parents for a few days. We arrived exhausted, and so my bedtime prayers were a quick "Thank You for a safe trip" and the usual "Please, dear Lord, be with me tomorrow."

The next afternoon, Grandma was pleased to have her only grandsons all to herself in the kitchen. And for me, here was a rare opportunity: time to indulge my love of piano playing.

I had brought a pile of long-neglected sheet music with me: my favorites and some I knew my father would enjoy. Shortly after I began to play, Father came in and sat in a living-room chair near the piano. He listened a minute, then pointed to a book on the music rack and said, "Play something out of that."

My father was a longtime fan of the Lawrence Welk television show, and the book he indicated was a collection of ragtime songs arranged by Tiny Little, who played piano on the show in its early days. Ragtime was my favorite kind of music and I'd had the book for several years. I had tried diligently to learn the songs, but with little formal training and even less natural ability, I hadn't been very successful.

I played the one song in the book that, with a lot of effort, I had mastered, and then I started to set the book aside. I knew the other songs were beyond my skill.

"Oh, play another one," said Father.

I looked through the book. Perhaps there was one other song I might be able to bluff my way through. I tried it and found I could play it almost perfectly, surely the best I'd ever done. Surprised and encouraged, I tried one more song . . . and then another, until I'd played—passably—the whole ragtime book.

My father enjoyed my ragtime recital, enjoyed it in a quiet

way. I could tell he was feeling tired, but I didn't realize at the time that he wasn't feeling well. There was no way for me to know the shock that lay ahead. My father died of heart failure the next morning.

I was where I needed to be for the next week, and when I returned home after Father's funeral I was tired and sad. But I had to resume the farm chores, and maybe that was just as well, for the work took my mind off my sorrow.

Finally, a few weeks later, I found time for a few minutes of recreational piano playing. I dug out the ragtime book, thinking, *Now that I know all these songs, I'll just play straight through this book.* I first played the one song I'd always been able to play. Then I went on to the other familiar one. I didn't play it very well. And how about the rest of the songs, the ones I'd sailed through that last afternoon with Father? Well, those songs were once again as far beyond me as they'd always been, my fingers utterly incapable of playing the notes my eyes were reading.

You might think this sudden return to incompetence would have saddened me. But it didn't. Instead, I felt consoled, even happy. Clearly God had given me a momentary gift, the chance to play gladdening songs for my father in his final hours. I closed the ragtime book and put it back in the piano bench, knowing more than ever that God is loving and kind.

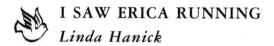

I SAW ERICA RUNNING
Linda Hanick

Our daughter, Erica, came into this world blind. Later, grave medical problems followed. Erica was almost four when it became clear she was dying. As Jack and I kept vigil at her hospital bedside, our prayers for her healing gradually became prayers for wisdom and acceptance.

Then Jack looked at me searchingly. "Linda," he said, "we should do more than pray to God about Erica. We need to talk to Erica about God."

I knew he was right. Erica was afraid, afraid of dying.

Despite her pain, I sensed she was holding on to us because we were the surest love she knew.

Cupping her tiny hands, we told her that God's love was so much greater than ours, and that she had to try to let go—of this hospital room, this bed, even us.

"Where you are going is a safe place, more beautiful and full of love than anything you've ever known . . ."

In my mind I saw Erica running, skipping over emerald grass through fields of rainbow-colored flowers. Her golden hair blazed in the sunlight. Her voice was laughter, and her eyes were like the sky, cloudless and blue. She was no longer blind.

A nurse came by to record Erica's vital signs. Though it was clear Erica's physical condition remained the same, I sensed a change, something deep in her spirit.

I was about to tell Jack when he said, "You know, just before the nurse came in I had the strongest image. I saw Erica, so vividly, skipping and running across a field of beautiful flowers. She was laughing. And her eyes were clear and blue as the sky."

THE AWAKENING
Michelle Yates

During the early morning hours of a warm night in June 1987, I was asleep in our home when something caused me to awaken. At first I thought I was dreaming. But no, I was sure I was awake, and still I heard it. Music. Beautiful, melodic strumming. I got up to check if someone had left a radio or TV on, but that wasn't it. I looked in on our four children to see if any of them was up playing a record. But all were sound asleep— except for our two-year-old, Jeriel, who was staring out the window.

"Jeriel, what are you doing?"

He turned toward me, his blue eyes wide. "Mommy, I hear songs."

I crouched down by his curly blond head and looked out the window, but I saw nothing, just the leaves on the tree. I picked him up. "Sweetheart, I hear it too. But let's try to go back to sleep." As I carried him back to bed and plumped up his Donald Duck pillow, my heart pounded. What *was* it?

Back in our bedroom I woke my husband, Michael. "Do you hear the music?" I asked. Groggily he shook his head and was soon snoring again.

The beautiful strumming became louder. Then it stopped, and a lively high-pitched voice began to sing, coming from the direction of our fenced-in, above-ground swimming pool. I clearly heard the words:

> *"In all things give Him praise,*
> *In all your days give Him your praise.*
> *He alone is worthy of your praise.*
> *Though you be racked with pain,*
> *Still proclaim He is Lord*
> *And give Him praise . . ."*

Next morning, as bright sunshine filled the house, and Mike went off to his job as an electronics engineer at the Highland Park Chrysler plant, I wondered if it had been a dream. Then as I poured cornflakes, Jeriel asked, "Mommy, who was that singing last night?"

I caught my breath, my mind whirling. Jeriel was soon rolling his little car across the breakfast table, but I continued to wonder. The message had sounded like what I'd always thought the singing of angels would be, and I've always believed in angels, God's messengers. But if it was indeed the music of angels, what could it mean? Jeriel and I were the only ones, apparently, who had heard anything. I just didn't know what to make of the strange experience.

Two months later, on Wednesday, August 19, 1987, Jeriel was so wound up that he didn't want to nap. Always a climber, he was up on the sofa back, then on my kitchen counters. Finally he crawled next to me on my bed, laid his head on my chest, and then looked up. "Game, Mommy." It was a little amusement we enjoyed. I pointed to his eye and said, "Eye, eye," then to his nose, "nose, nose," and on to his mouth, teeth, and cheeks. I brushed my fingers through his soft blond curls and he laughed. Then, as always, I ended by saying, "Mommy loves you, Jeriel; Jesus loves you." He kissed me and said, "Jerielly loves you, and Jesus loves you too."

He relaxed and, looking at the picture over my bed, whispered, "Mommy, that's Jesus." I was thrilled. I had been trying to teach him that for months.

At supper Jeriel was the clown as usual. He had learned a new giggle, and all of us had fun in our attempts to mimic him. Afterward, the children asked to go swimming. I wasn't feeling well, so Mike said he would watch them while I rested on the sofa. Soon I dozed off.

Suddenly I was wakened. "Mommy, Jeriel fell in the pool!" It was six-year-old Athena, her eyes wide in terror.

I leapt up and raced out the back door. There on the pool's wooden deck Jeriel lay wet and motionless. Mike was bending over him, frantically giving him CPR. "Call the police!" Mike yelled.

In minutes, Mike and our landlord, who lives nearby, were putting Jeriel into our van to rush him to the Saline Hospital. Before leaving, Mike brokenly explained that while he was in the basement getting some toys, he hadn't noticed that Jeriel had slipped out of the house and climbed the pool fence.

Athena, five-year-old Gabriel, and three-year-old Josiah were crying. "Jerielly is dead!" screamed Athena. "I don't want my baby brother to be dead!"

"We don't know that," I soothed. Then I sat them down. "Look, Jeriel is in the hands of God. We must trust Him. Now let's pray for Jeriel to be strong. We are a family, and must stay together in Jesus, no matter what."

I put our children in the care of neighbors and rushed to the hospital. There Mike and I waited, gripping each other's hands.

When the doctor appeared, her face was grave. "We finally got a faint heartbeat," she said. "But"—she touched my shoulder—"you must remember, there may be some brain damage."

"I don't care," I cried. "I just want my baby back alive."

Finally they let us see Jeriel. He was lying in the trauma room with machines beeping. I brushed wet curls from his closed eyes. How small and helpless he looked. Soon a helicopter came to whisk him to Mott Hospital in Ann Arbor, which the doctor said was the best pediatric center in the area.

Mike went home for Jeriel's Donald Duck pillow and his favorite shirt and pants, for Jeriel to wear when he came home.

Then we waited at Mott Hospital. I felt as if I were in a bad dream, and I kept asking God, "Please, wake me up."

Finally, the doctor came out. "Your son is in a deep coma. His brain has been without oxygen long enough to suffer damage. To what extent we don't know."

Mike and I turned and held each other, and prayed. Friends and relatives came to sit with us and pray. I sensed God's sweet Holy Spirit surrounding us all.

Two days later the doctor came in with Jeriel's test results. "It's not promising," he said. "Your son is ninety percent brain dead. He might live on or die in a few days or weeks. We can't tell."

I began sobbing. My friend Glenda put her arm around me. "Michelle, you have to give Jeriel to Jesus."

I stared at her. *No,* I thought, *God has turned things around before for me. He can heal Jeriel too.* Later that day as I held Jeriel's hand and talked to him, he drew my hand up to his heart. My spirits soared. He could hear me!

But every report was worse than the one before. On Sunday night, after Jeriel had been in a coma for four days, the doctor offered no hope. "It could be," he said, "that the time may soon come when we should turn off his life-support system." He looked up at us gravely. "We could keep him going, or do you want us just to let him go? We will need to know your decision soon."

Mike felt it would be best to let Jeriel go but I could not think of it.

Rachel, one of the many friends who had comforted us, stayed with me in the waiting room that night. I took off my shoes, lay down on a chair that converted into a bed, and finally went to sleep. But then I dreamed that I rose from my bed and walked into Jeriel's room. His body was attached to all sorts of needles and tubes. I leaned over and whispered in his ear, "Jeriel, my little sweetheart, I have always tried to teach you to obey Mommy and Daddy. Well, now there is another who is calling you. I told you that above all others we are to obey our Heavenly Father. And if He is calling you, you must go to Him."

I picked up my child, and to my surprise, all the needles and tubes fell from him. I cradled his limp body in my arms. As I stood crying, I heard someone call my name. I looked up. It was Jesus! His eyes were full of compassion.

"O Father, heal him, please, whether it be by his living or going home with You," I begged. But I already knew the answer. "Father," I continued, "when Jeriel was born, we dedicated him to You. He is Yours. I have always prayed that Your will be done."

He smiled. "Daughter, I love you and will give you strength and comfort."

I held Jeriel close, kissed him, and laid him at Jesus' feet. I stepped back and the Lord picked him up. Instantly Jeriel awoke. He looked up at the Lord, grinned, and said, "Hi, Jesus!"

The Lord held Jeriel out to me, and once more we played our little game. I touched his ear, his eye, his nose, mouth, and cheeks, and finished as always by saying, "Mommy loves you; Jesus loves you." He kissed me and said, "Jerielly loves you, and Jesus loves you too."

Then Jesus, with Jeriel in His arms, began to walk out of the room. The Lord motioned me to come. We walked along the darkened hospital corridor, took the elevator down to the lobby, and went past the reception desk to the double glass doors of the hospital entrance. Outside, instead of the courtyard, there was a hill covered with deep green grass, and the sky was pure and clear.

I stood inside the door, watching in awe as Jesus set Jeriel down. He took off in a run for the hill, stopped, picked a flower, and counted the petals, his voice crystal clear: "One, two, three, nine!" (He still hadn't learned to count.) "See," Jesus said to me, "he is alive. All who are in My care are alive and growing here."

Then He and Jeriel walked over the hill together. Once, Jeriel looked back, smiled, and called, "Mommy, I love you and will always be at your side." Then they were gone and I went back to sleep on my makeshift bed in the waiting room.

In the morning when I awoke, Rachel asked me a startling question: "Did you know you were walking in your sleep last night?" She went on to tell me I had left the room, walked down the corridor, and taken the elevator.

"I couldn't have," I insisted. .

"No," she said, "you did some walking all right." Rachel pointed to my feet. "Okay, then explain why your shoes are on. You took them off when you went to bed. Now each is on the wrong foot."

I looked down. She was right.

Then the night nurse stuck her head into the room and said to me, "I hope I didn't disturb you last night—when you were in Jeriel's room, praying."

I was stunned. I had thought it all a dream. And yet . . .

Had it been only two months since I'd wondered if I'd had another dream—the music of the angels? But that music had been real. I had heard it. Jeriel had heard it. Why? Now, looking back, I knew. God was preparing us. But last night? It must have been the hand of God as well.

I got up and went into Jeriel's room, now half expecting to find his bed empty. But he was there, still connected to the tubes and the hissing machine. Yet something was different. As I looked down at him, somehow Jeriel was not the same. Then I knew: Jeriel was gone; only his body lived on.

From that moment on I was at ease. I did not have to insist on keeping his life-support system running; I could let go.

But Mike and I didn't have to make that decision. In forty-eight hours Jeriel's heart stopped beating. And for the first time since the accident, he was smiling.

 ## EVERYTHING WILL BE ALL RIGHT
Ruth Whittet

When the doctor told us Jim had cancer, we could hardly grasp the words. This was something that just didn't happen to young marrieds, certainly not to *us!* It couldn't happen to a strong, healthy young man just beginning a productive life—not to a father of three small children.

But in some numbing, inexplicable way it had, and as Jim and I began to take it in, we did what I suppose most people do at such times—we turned to God in panic. Up till then we'd made feeble attempts to attend church, never really settling on one denomination, but trying first one and then another. Now in real earnest we began to explore spiritually — studying, praying, reading the Bible together.

One night I lay in bed beside my sleeping husband, unable to stop my thoughts. The house was dark and still, the children peacefully asleep. Through a crack under the window shade the stars were visibly twinkling in the sky. And I lay there cold with fear. My sweet, gentle, handsome young husband was going to die. "O God, help us, help him, help me to help him. Give us a miracle, Lord," I prayed.

And there, in the upper left corner of the room, the miracle began. It was a ball of light, whirling, coming closer, brighter and brighter, showering sparks around the room like a Fourth of July sparkler, moving, but with a powerful stillness like God's universe.

Blinking, I sat up in bed and still the light was there. Then I heard the words, tremendous and gentle as the light that seemed now to fill the house.

"Everything will be all right."

Five words, but somehow I knew that God Himself had spoken them.

Often in the following two years those words were all I had to hang onto. For in spite of repeated surgery and radiation treatments, Jim—to the outward eye anyway—was growing worse, the pain ever harder to bear, the once tall, strong body thin and wasted.

Then came that special night. For three days past, with every waking breath Jim had begged me to help in withstanding the pain. Now at last he was sleeping peacefully. But, exhausted as I was, somehow I couldn't go to bed.

The children were afraid but very perceptive. They did everything quietly and with an understanding obedience that said, "We know what's happening and will not add to the upset." After kissing their daddy and me goodnight, they had gone quickly to sleep without the usual rituals of the bedtime story and trips to the bathroom.

Some months before, we had moved Jim's bed to the living room. As I sat beside him there, watching him breathing regularly, his pleading voice quieted, I felt a wonderful sense of peace. Once again, as I had so many times in the last two years, I seemed to hear those words, "Everything will be all right."

Still I did not go to my own bed in the next room but sat beside him, silently reading the Bible and praying. I wanted so much to ask God to erase all of this, to let it be a bad dream. But it wasn't a dream. It was stubbornly, horribly real.

Finally, after two hours of praying, then sobbing, then reading, then hoping, then daring not to hope, I relinquished my hold on this person I loved more than anything else in the world. I said the prayer that I now believe gave my husband relief from his suffering: "O God, take him if You must, but don't let him suffer anymore." Then I kissed him, went into my room, and fell asleep immediately.

For several months preceding that night Jim had awakened me at three o'clock each morning to talk and pray with him. So it was habit, I suppose, that called me from sleep that night at 3:00 A.M. as usual. But it was what happened before I awoke that is so hard to put into words. For many years I didn't even try. Maybe I was selfish, wanting to hold onto it for myself, receiving comfort from it. Maybe I was afraid people would think me insane or self-deluding. But I have never been more certain of anything than of this event.

Suddenly I was wide awake instantly, as if my body were tensed for the unexpected. I lay there listening for any sound from the living room. I did not get up immediately but waited to absorb a Presence that once again seemed to fill the room. I looked around, expecting another bright light, for I felt the same exhilaration I had that other time. But there was no light, no voice. I lay there waiting and all at once I was remembering the dream I had just had. I closed my eyes and experienced the dream over again.

My husband's mother, who had passed away almost eight years before, and a good friend of the family, Aunt Charlotte, who had died some years before that, were standing in our living room. Together they looked down at the bed where my husband lay. They talked and laughed, joyously greeting their loved one. Although I couldn't hear their words, I understood they were telling Jim that they had come to take him home with them.

At first he seemed to be resisting; then just as easily and nonchalantly he nodded. By his acceptance he seemed to say that he knew he could no longer take care of his family, that he could leave them in God's hands. There was no more pain reflected on Jim's face. He got up, looked at the worn, pain-lined face of the body that was no longer his, took an arm of each woman, and together they left the house.

I rose from my bed and tiptoed to the door of the living room. Jim's body lay on the bed, strangely quiet.

There, in the silence of death, in a small house like thousands of other small houses in the world, I felt no sadness, no immediate grief, only humility and a sense of the reality of God. For He had visited me with His love and a promise, and had come again to show me the fulfillment — everything was all right, now and forever.

THE PHONE CALL
Linda A. Fuesz

Outside the bedroom window on this Sunday morning in July, the birds were just awaking. The air had the freshness that seems to exist only in those moments before the sun rises.

Inside, two people lay side by side. For forty years they had shared their lives and been attuned to each other, but never as intensely as now. For fourteen months, since the surgery that revealed the presence of cancer in his body, their marriage had taken on another dimension. The possibility that their time together on earth was drawing to a close made every moment precious.

She'd found herself studying his face when he wasn't aware of her presence. She wanted to memorize every feature: the eyes revealing the kindness inside the man, the large nose that the family lovingly teased him about, the mouth that smiled so easily or was so often pursed for whistling.

He'd been spending more hours lying on the couch or out in his hammock under a tree. Often he'd been lost in thought with a faraway look in his eyes. She longed to know what he was thinking, but to ask would be an intrusion on the thoughts which seemed to be one of the last things he could control as his body weakened.

She was in a deep sleep. He was beginning to stir. His first movements brought her quickly from her slumber, and she was immediately wide awake.

"Do you need some help?" she asked.

"No, I think I can take care of it," he replied as he reached for the urinal beside the bed. Lately, he'd not had the strength to walk down the hall to the bathroom when he awoke during the night.

After several minutes of fumbling, he admitted he would need her help after all.

"This is so ridiculous!" he said as they settled back into their warm bed. How difficult it was for him—indeed, for anyone—to have to depend on another for even the most basic needs.

"It's not at all ridiculous," she reassured him.

They were drifting off to sleep again. His arms were around her when suddenly he raised his head off the pillow and looked intently toward the east window of the bedroom.

"What is that bright light?" he asked, his voice intense.

She looked at him and then toward the window. "It's just the sun coming up."

"No, it's—"

He struggled to speak. His eyes showed that he'd seen something he wanted to tell her about, but he could not bring out the words. At that moment he drifted into unconsciousness.

Was this the moment she had been fearing? Quickly making sure he was carefully covered up, she slipped out of bed, reached for her robe, and climbed the stairs to the bedroom where their youngest son and his wife were sleeping. The doctor was telephoned, then their youngest daughter and her husband, who lived a short distance away.

The doctor confirmed what they had sensed already, that he had only hours to live.

The hours passed. The members of the family took turns sitting at the side of his bed. Even though he was in a coma, they felt that he would sense their presence and their love. It was she who was there beside him when the telephone in the hall rang. It rang again. Everyone else seemed to be in a different part of the house. Though the family had protected her from calls that morning, she knew she must answer this one. She picked up the phone just as the others were rounding the corner to answer for her.

"Hello?" she said.

On the other end a small, weak voice said, "Don't be afraid—the Lord's blessings are with you."

Her mind raced as she searched her memory trying to identify the strange voice. She was unable to respond because there was something so odd about the call. The look on her face was one of confusion as she held out the phone to her son-in-law.

"Hello?" he spoke into the receiver. Then he turned to her. "There's no one there now. Who was it, Mother?"

"I don't know, dear. It was a voice that sounded weak, far away, strange."

As the phone was replaced on its cradle, her daughter-in-law was the first to ask, "Did you see it, Mother? Did you see the phone? Did you see the phone glowing?"

And surely, they had all witnessed the strange phenomenon. There they were, a wife and mother of forty years surrounded by members of her family; a statistician with a master's degree, a statistician with a bachelor's degree, a plant pathologist with a doctoral degree, and a businessman, all standing in the dim hallway by the golden wall-phone. The very moment she had handed the phone to her son-in-law, the glowing had ceased and the caller was gone.

The glowing phone with the strange message did not change the course of the morning. When the moment of death came a few hours later, she was sitting, once again, at his side. She was watching the slow pulsing artery in his neck when the pulsing simply stopped. She remained near when the doctor pronounced death, and then she went downstairs to the basement. To watch her husband leave home for the last time was more than she could bear.

It has been seven years since that morning in July. I share this story with you today as an encouragement. You see, the man who died was my father. And my mother, who had so dreaded his death and was frightened by what life would be like without him, walked gallantly through the difficult days when her family returned to their own homes and their own lives. The two-story family home which she'd been sure would never offer her comfort without her husband became a place of solace and refuge after all. She never experienced any fear of staying alone. Mother immediately took over the upkeep of the yard, the house, the car, the finances, all duties which Daddy had performed and in which she had taken little interest. She not only handled these things, but accomplished them with skill and with a rewarding sense of fulfillment as well.

I believe that Mother was changed and strengthened by the mysterious voice on the glowing telephone.

And we, her children, have observed with amazement and humble thanksgiving how faithful the Lord is to His children when they are in need. We will not know until we meet the Lord face to face what wonderful bright light my father was seeing just before he lost consciousness. Nor will we know who was on the other end of the glowing phone. Yet the words "Don't be afraid—the Lord's blessings are with you" continue to have their impact. Is it not possible that the Lord, who understands every desire of our hearts, had compassion on my mother and allowed my father a final phone call?

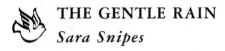

THE GENTLE RAIN
Sara Snipes

For Robert and me, rain was always heaven-sent. During our courtship there was not much money for entertainment; however, we always enjoyed walking together—particularly in the rain. The rain poured continually on our wedding day. For the next twenty-one years of our marriage Robert often told of stopping for gas in my little town of Watkinsville, Georgia, on the way to our wedding. Since Robert was from south Georgia, no one knew him. The owner of the gas station laughed and told Robert about some poor nut who was getting married in this downpour. Some poor nut indeed!

For our wedding, Robert had had an inscription engraved inside my ring, but I didn't know how it read until I removed the ring as he checked us into our honeymoon suite. There I saw the words, *Because You Walked With Me in the Rain.*

Through the years of child rearing, losing parents through death, moving, and worrying about jobs—no matter the problem—our faith in God remained steadfast, and we always took comfort in His word, just like it says, "My words shall fall upon you like the gentle rain" (Deuteronomy 32:2, TLB).

Then one night Robert died suddenly from a heart attack. Soon family and friends gathered around me, but after they left, I didn't want to go to bed. I felt so alone. I wandered outside and stood on the front porch. The night was quiet, the sky was clear. And then, for only a few remarkable seconds, there came the familiar, comforting, reassuring sound—of raindrops splattering on the sidewalk before me.

WHEN I SAW HEAVEN IN MOTHER'S EYES
Julia Tinkey

There's something about a hospital in the dead of night that is different from anything else—muted sighs and stirrings, the light from the nurses' station at the end of the floor.

I sat by Mother's bed, watching. There wasn't much else I could do. Jean Hudson, the night nurse, was in and out, checking Mother's pulse and blood pressure.

In fact, as the minutes crawled past, I grew more and more sensitive to the impulse that had made me leave my husband and our three children asleep and drive to the hospital at midnight. We'd known for six weeks that Mother was dying. Ever since surgery had revealed inoperable cancer, I'd spent part of each day at her side. This night I *had to be with her.*

It was true, the last few days she'd been failing rapidly, in much pain, drifting in and out of a coma. Several times the doctor had been on the verge of telling her that further treatment was useless—but we all hesitated. All her life Mother had been such an active person, teaching at the high school, running the farm, doing office work for dad's pulpwood business, raising five children, and cheerfully taking on jobs at church. To be able to fight now, however vainly, we felt was important to her.

She still had not moved nor opened her eyes since I arrived. I repeated again the prayer I had said so often in that room. It was that Mother not have to go with drugs numbing that close harmony of mind to mind and heart to heart we had always had in our family. As I had done daily the past six weeks, I prayed that Mother—who had served God so faithfully these seventy years—be allowed to come to Him in dignity and acceptance and peace.

"Julia!" Mother stirred on the bed. "Are you there, Julia?"

I assured her that I was, and she asked me to come closer. She wanted to apologize, she said, for having been so difficult (which of course she hadn't).

Her eyes opened; they looked straight into mine. "The doctor told me. And, Julia, it's all right. I've left it up to God. I'm in God's hands now, and it is so wonderful."

As she was saying this, she seemed bathed in light. As I stared at her, the mysterious radiance enveloped me as well; I felt as if I were drowning in the love and joy on her face.

I realized that she was smiling and I smiled back—but I could not express this awareness enough through smiles; it seemed that my body must burst with the fullness of that instant.

The instant stretched into minutes and the minutes into almost an hour as we looked at each other, exposed and filled with the living presence of God. I felt that Mother was seeing a world beyond the physical one, and that I was *almost* there with her.

I said to her, "Do you mean, Mother, that you see God?" and she answered, "Yes, Julia, face to face, and it is so important that everyone know. Tell Murray, Carol, Miriam, George," naming my brothers and sisters. "It's so wonderful!"

She seemed so alert, so like her former self that in frustration I almost shouted at her. "What's so wonderful? Tell me!"

"Millions and millions of people," she began slowly. "So many millions . . . and all on different levels. There's light . . . light everywhere . . . so much light!"

Her eyes seemed so full of love and they never left mine. Her voice remained strong as she continued. "Things get between us and God. Tell them all not to let things separate them from God. I've been so concerned with my own little problems and desires. Tell them, Julia—the glory of the Lord—it is wonderful!"

They were the last words that Mother spoke. Her eyes closed, but the smile did not fade.

PISGAH
—*Willard Wattles*

By every ebb of the river-side
My heart to God hath daily cried;
By every shining shingle-bar
I found the pathway of a star;
By every dizzy mountain height
He touches me for cleaner sight,
As Moses' face hath shined to see
His intimate divinity.
Through desert sand I stumbling pass
To death's cool plot of friendly grass,
Knowing each painful step I trod
Hath brought me daily home to God.

HE
Orders
HIS ANGELS

For he orders his angels to protect you wherever you go. They will steady you with their hands to keep you from stumbling against the rocks on the trail.
                                        —PSALM 91:11–12, TLB

NOW THE DAY IS OVER
—Sabine Baring-Gould

Now the day is over,
Night is drawing nigh,
Shadows of the evening
Steal across the sky.

. . . .

Jesus give the weary
Calm and sweet repose,
With thy tenderest blessing
May our eyelids close.

Grant to little children
Visions bright of thee,
Guard the sailors tossing
On the deep blue sea. ﹀

Through the long night-watches
May thy angels spread
Their white wings above me,
Watching round my bed.

When the morning wakens,
Then may I arise
Pure and fresh and sinless
In thy holy eyes.

THE DAY WE SAW THE ANGELS
S. Ralph Harlow

It was not Christmas, it was not even wintertime, when the
event occurred that for me threw sudden new light on the
ancient angel tale. It was a glorious spring morning, and my
wife, Marion, and I were walking through the newly budded
birches and maples near Ballardvale, Massachusetts.

Now, I realize that this, like any account of personal experience, is only as valid as the good sense and honesty of the person
relating it. What can I say about myself? That I am a scholar
who shuns guesswork and admires scientific investigation? That
I have an A.B. from Harvard, an M.A from Columbia, a PH.D
from Hartford Theological Seminary? That I have never been
subject to hallucinations? All this is true, and yet I doubt that
such credentials can influence the belief of another.

In the long run, each of us must sift what comes to us from
others through his own life experience, his view of the universe.
And so I will simply tell my story.

The little path on which Marion and I walked that morning
was spongy to our steps and we held hands with the sheer
delight of life. It was May, and because it was the examination
reading period for students at Smith College where I was a
professor, we were able to get away for a few days to visit
Marion's parents.

We frequently took walks in the country, and we especially
loved the spring after a hard New England winter, for it is then
that the fields and the woods are radiant with new life. This day
we were especially happy and peaceful; we chatted sporadically,
with great gaps of satisfying silence between our sentences.

Then from behind us we heard the murmur of muted voices,
and I said to Marion, "We have company in the woods this
morning."

Marion nodded and turned to look. We saw nothing, but the
voices were coming nearer—at a faster pace than we were
walking, and we knew that the strangers would soon overtake
us. Then we perceived that the sounds were not only behind us
but above us, and we looked up.

How can I describe what we felt? Is it possible to tell of the
surge of exaltation that ran through us? Is it possible to record
this phenomenon in objective accuracy and yet be credible?

For about ten feet above us, and slightly to our left, was a
floating group of glorious, beautiful creatures that glowed with
spiritual beauty. We stopped and stared as they passed above
us.

There were six of them, young beautiful women dressed in
flowing white garments and engaged in earnest conversation. If
they were aware of our existence they gave no indication of it.
Their faces were perfectly clear to us, and one woman, slightly

older than the rest, was especially beautiful. Her dark hair was pulled back in what today we would call a ponytail which appeared to be bound at the back of her head. She was talking intently to a younger spirit who looked up into her face.

Neither Marion nor I could understand their words although their voices were clearly heard.

They seemed to float past us, and their graceful motion was as gentle and peaceful as the morning itself. As they passed, their conversation grew fainter until it faded out entirely, and we stood transfixed on the spot, still holding hands. Then we looked at each other, each wondering if the other also had seen.

There was a fallen birch tree beside the path. We sat down on it, and I said, "Marion, what did you see and hear? Tell me exactly."

She knew my intent—to see if I had been the victim of hallucination. And her reply was identical in every respect to what I'd seen and heard.

I have related this story with the same respect for truth as I would on the witness stand. But I know how incredible it sounds.

Perhaps I can claim no more for it than that it has had a deep effect on our own lives. For this experience of over thirty years ago greatly altered our thinking. Once both Marion and I were somewhat skeptical about the absolute accuracy of the details at the birth of Christ. The story, as recorded by St. Luke, tells of an angel appearing to "shepherds abiding in the field" and after the shepherds had been told of the birth, "suddenly there was with the angel a multitude of the heavenly host praising God, and saying, Glory to God in the highest" (Luke 2:8–14).

As a child I accepted this multitude as literal heavenly personages. Then I went through a period when I felt that they were merely symbols injected into a legend. Today, after the experience at Ballardvale, Marion and I are no longer skeptical. We believe that St. Luke records a genuine objective experience told in wonder by those who lived it.

Once, too, we puzzled over the Christian insistence that we have "bodies" other than our normal flesh and blood ones. We were like the doubter of whom St. Paul wrote: "But some man will say, How are the dead raised up? and with what body do they come?" (1 Corinthians 15:35).

In the thirty years since that bright May morning, his answer has rung for us with joyous conviction.

"There are also celestial bodies, and bodies terrestrial: but the glory of the celestial is one, and the glory of the terrestrial is another. . . . So also is the resurrection of the dead. . . . It is sown a natural body; it is raised a spiritual body. There is a natural body, and there is a spiritual body. . . . And as we have borne the image of the earthy, we shall also bear the image of the heavenly"(1 Corinthians 15:40–49).

All of us, I think, hear the angels for a little while at Christmastime. But we reject the very possibility that what the shepherds saw two thousand years ago was part of the reality that presses close every day of our lives.

And yet there is no reason to shrink from this knowledge. Since Marion and I began to be aware of the host of heaven all about us, our lives have been filled with a wonderful hope. Phillips Brooks, the great Episcopal bishop, expressed it beautifully:

"Hold fast to yourself the sympathy and companionship of the unseen worlds. No doubt it is best for us now that they should be unseen. It cultivates in us that higher perception that we call 'faith.' But who can say that the time will not come when, even to those who live here upon earth, the unseen worlds shall no longer be unseen?"

The experience at Ballardvale, added to the convictions of my Christian faith, gives me not only a feeling of assurance about the future, but a sense of adventure toward it too.

THE SNAKEBITE
Debbie Durrance

We had just finished Sunday dinner when our twelve-year-old son, Mark, asked if he and his dog, Bo, could go out into the field beyond our house for a while. "Just be careful," my husband told him. It was the advice Bobby always gave our children whenever they went out alone, especially in the three

years since we'd moved thirty miles out into the brushland of
southwestern Florida. Several of our animals had been bitten by
rattlesnakes.

As I cleared away the dinner dishes, I watched Mark and Bo
race off through the orange and lemon trees of our private oasis.
Mark had become so self-reliant out here in the country, I
thought.

I took my time with the dishes, enjoying the slow Sunday
afternoon, and was just finishing up when I heard the living-
room door open. Suddenly our older son, Buddy, yelled,
"Mark, what's wrong?" I threw down the dish towel and ran
toward the living room just as Mark gasped, "I—I've been
rattlesnake-bit—" There was a dull thud. When I got there,
Mark was on the floor, unconscious. "Go get your dad. Hurry!"
I said to Buddy.

I pulled off Mark's shoe; his foot had already swollen into a
large, ugly purple mass. There was a musky odor about him,
the same odor we'd noticed the times our animals had been
bitten by rattlesnakes. In seconds, Bobby rushed in and grabbed
Mark up in his arms. "Come on," he said. "We've got to get
him to the emergency center."

We ran and climbed into the cab of Bobby's work truck. I
held Mark on my lap, Buddy sat in the middle, and Bobby
drove. "O God," I prayed, "help us." It was seventeen miles to
the emergency center, and every minute counted.

Mark was unconscious, and convulsions jerked his body. I
tried to hold him still, with his face close to mine. As long as
I could feel his breath against my cheek, I knew he was still
alive. But the soft flutters were becoming weaker and less
frequent.

"Hurry, Bobby—please hurry!" I pleaded as he frantically
passed car after car. Buddy sat in the center, quietly struggling
to hold his brother's legs. None of us dared say it, but we all
knew we were in a race with death.

As we neared the business section, steam started to seep out
from under the hood of the truck. The motor was overheating.
About a mile from the clinic, the motor began to pop and
sputter.

I glanced over at Bobby. What would we do if the motor
stopped? But before I could get the words out, Bobby had to

brake for a slower vehicle and the motor cut off completely. I clutched Mark to me, trying to hold on to whatever life was left. We were right in the middle of traffic. Cars were pulling around us and honking their horns. Bobby jumped out and tried to flag down one of the motorists, but the cars just sped around him. "Why won't they stop?" Buddy sighed.

Desperate by now, Bobby ran over and pulled Mark from my arms. He carried him out to the rear of the car, where the other drivers could see him, but still the cars kept going by. Finally one old compact car stopped. The driver appeared to be a Haitian farm worker, and he didn't understand English. But he could tell we needed help.

"Thank you, thank you . . ." Bobby shouted as he pulled open the door and pushed Buddy in the backseat. Then he laid Mark down beside him and waved the driver off as I jumped in the front.

"We have to get to the emergency center" I cried, but the driver's questioning look told me he didn't understand. I pointed in the direction we should go.

As we pulled away, I glanced back at Bobby standing in the street. There was no room for him in the small car and our truck was blocking traffic, but I wished he could be with me.

At the emergency center, medical technicians started working on Mark immediately, trying to stabilize his condition. They started fluids and began artificial respiration. But soon after Bobby arrived, the emergency technicians told us they had done all they could and were transferring Mark to Naples Community Hospital, where Dr. Michael Nycum would meet us.

By the time we arrived at the hospital, Mark had stopped breathing twice and had gone into a coma. For the next twelve hours we waited and prayed while the doctors and nurses worked constantly with him. We could tell by the looks on their faces that they didn't expect him to make it.

"Folks, about the only thing the little fellow has going for him is his heart—and that's under tremendous strain," Dr. Nycum told us.

We watched helplessly during the next twenty-four hours as the venom attacked every part of his body. His eyes swelled so tight that all we could see were the ends of his eyelashes. His leg was so swollen the doctors had to make long slashes along it to relieve the pressure on the blood vessels. And still they were afraid they might have to amputate.

Then, miraculously, Mark passed the crisis point and began to improve a little. He was still in a coma, and certainly not out of danger, but the swelling began to go down.

After that, each day brought improvement. On Thursday, Bobby and I sat there beside Mark's bed. We were drained, exhausted, prayed out. I was sitting in a chair close to him, holding his hand, when I thought I felt a movement. But no, I told myself, it was probably my imagination. Yet a moment later, there it was again, a faint fluttering of the small hand inside mine.

"Bobby," I said, sitting up and reaching across to him, "Bobby! Mark moved—he moved!"

Bobby summoned the nurses and doctor. Mark was coming out of the coma.

"Mom . . . Mom . . ." he moaned.

"Yes, honey, we're here." The words caught in my throat.

"Dad . . ."

"Yes, Son . . ."

His eyes opened now as he looked over at Bobby. "Dad . . . are you mad at me?"

"What do you mean?" Bobby tried to laugh, but it came out a little ragged. "Of course I'm not mad at you."

"I was afraid you'd be mad at me for being so careless."

Bobby reached over and patted Mark on the head. "We're just thankful you're getting better. But what happened, Son? Do you feel like telling us?"

The nurses and Dr. Nycum moved a little closer.

"Well, Bo and I spotted a bird in a cabbage palm and, well, I guess I wasn't paying too much attention to where I was going. I was looking at the bird and jumped over the ditch . . . and my foot landed on something that moved when I hit it.

"And then it was like something slammed down hard on my foot, and my leg started getting real hot. When I looked down, I saw a big rattler had hold of my shoe—it was biting on my foot. It was hurting so bad and Bo was barking and jumping at the snake, but it wouldn't let go. Then Bo jumped on the snake and tore into its head. It let go and crawled off into the bushes.

"Dad, I tried to remember what you said to do if we ever got snakebit, but I was hurting so bad, and getting weak and dizzy. I was a long way from the house, and I knew none of you would hear if I called . . ."

"But where were you, Mark?" Bobby asked.

"Out in the field, a long ways from the house. Out there next to the ditch in the field."

"But that's a third of a mile from the house. How did you get to the house?"

Dr. Nycum shook his head. "Medically speaking, it would have been impossible for him to have walked that far."

Bobby and I looked uncertainly at each other. There were also the thirteen steps up to our front door—he'd had to climb those too. I took a deep breath. After everything that had happened, I was almost afraid to ask, but I had to know, "How did you get back to the house, Mark?"

"Well, I remembered you and Dad saying that the more you moved, the quicker the poison would reach your heart, and I knew I couldn't run. But I was so scared, and all I wanted to do was get home. I probably would have run if I could have, but I couldn't because it hurt so bad. And then . . . Dad, there's something I have to tell you. About the man."

"The man? What man?" Bobby asked. "Was someone out there with you?"

"Yes—I mean, no—I mean, I don't know. All I know is that he carried me . . ."

"He carried you?"

"Yes, when I couldn't make it to the house. He picked me up." I could feel a tingle on the back of my neck.

"He talked to me in a real deep voice," Mark went on, "and told me that I was going to be real sick, but that I'd be all right."

"What did he look like?" I asked Mark shakily.

"I couldn't see his face, Mom. All I could see was that he had on a white robe, and his arms were real strong. He reached down and picked me up. And I was hurting so bad, I just sort of leaned my head over on him. He carried me to the house and up the steps. When he put me down, I held on to the door and turned around, and—"

His blue eyes stared into mine with an earnestness I'd never seen before. "All I could see was his back."

For a long time, none of us could speak; it was almost

more than we could take in. "God is our refuge and strength," I said to myself, "a very present help in trouble" (Psalm 46:1, RSV).

For most of my life I had believed that passage in the Bible by faith. Now I saw the proof of it.

"Mom . . . Dad . . ." Mark said, hesitating. "I know you may not believe me—"

"We believe you," I whispered as Bobby put his arm around me. "We believe you."

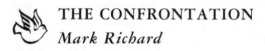

THE CONFRONTATION
Mark Richard

I had been in New York just a few weeks, having moved here from Virginia Beach, Virginia. The only apartment I could afford was in a bad neighborhood in the borough of Queens, where at night roaches skittered across the walls and the streets were filled with young toughs. After much prayer and searching, I found a temporary job in a restaurant in Manhattan's Greenwich Village.

The restaurant often closed at two or three in the morning, but because we had to count out the registers and clean up, we waiters were sometimes not able to leave until four. Then I had to cross several dark streets with my tips, all the money I had in the world, divided in different pockets and zippered in the lining of my jacket. The idea was, in case I was mugged, maybe the thieves would not take everything I had. I learned this ploy from my co-workers. While cleaning up, they would often swap tales of being held up on the way home—at knifepoint, gunpoint, or just by a hand thrust into a paper sack (and having to decide whether a weapon was really concealed within). I later learned from a police detective that generally there *is* a gun in the paper sack; muggers use the tactic so victims will not freeze with fear and fail to cooperate.

After leaving the restaurant I would catch the Seventh Avenue subway to Times Square, where I would transfer to the Number 7, the only train out to my neighborhood. At that hour, the Times Square subway station is a strangely quiet place. Long corridors connecting platforms are empty. There are blind turns. Great lengths of walkways are garishly lit with bare bulbs. It is a place of passage for the occasional late-night reveler, a retreat where the homeless sleep. And it is a place for those intent on criminal mischief, for the subways themselves provide getaways, and the tunnels a maze of hiding places.

One night I stood on a platform waiting for a train that seemed long overdue. I had been on my feet for ten hours serving a surly Saturday-evening crowd. At the other end of the platform were three young men. We seemed to be the only people in this place. Indeed, I felt as if we were the only people in this big city waiting underground for a train home.

After a while, I noticed that the three men were watching me. Were they sizing me up? I told myself I was just being paranoid from being tired, having about a hundred dollars in tips in my pockets, and being new to the city. Still, I moved a little way down the platform.

That was probably a mistake. Animals can detect fear in humans, and I am sure that experienced criminals can do the same thing. The three men moved down the platform, easing closer to me. Needless to say, I was whispering some quiet prayers and glancing at a stairway that would be my escape route if I had to make a run for it.

To avoid showing my fear, I concentrated on the tiles in the opposite wall across the subway tracks and looked down the darkened tube, hoping and praying the train would arrive. I became aware of how cavernous the entire structure was; in some ways its arches and ceilings reminded me of some cathedrals I had visited.

The three young men were now watching me closely and taking smaller steps to where I stood. Instead of fearing for my life, incredibly, I was wondering how I was going to pay my rent after being relieved of my money. I took another step toward the stairway leading up from the platform.

At this point I put everything into the Lord's hands. I was praying. I was sweating. In the adrenaline rush of fight-or-flight, I was preparing to run up the stairs when one of the men walked around me to the foot of the stairway, where he stood, arms crossed, staring at me.

Just as I was expecting them to demand my valuables, a

strange thing happened. From the stairway came a singing voice. It was so soft at first that it could have been just a note of a distant siren, but then I distinctly heard a couple of phrases. The song was in a language I did not understand. As the voice grew louder, it sounded like Latin. It was a soft male voice but strong and confident in its high reaches.

Our little platform drama halted. In fact, the man from whom I expected the demand, who only moments before seemed ready to speak, remained quiet, as if his words stuck in his throat. The voice approached us from the stairway, and now we could even hear slow, steady, heavy footsteps. My first instinct was to thank God for sending me an Irish cop on his beat singing a song from his days as an altar boy.

Apparently my companions did not share my perception of a possible rescue. Perhaps it was because the footfalls were taking so long to come to the top of the stairway. Perhaps it was the song itself. Perhaps, although the steps sounded heavy, the voice was so delicate that its owner would be little deterrent to crime. An arm reached for my jacket.

And there we stood, motionless, everyone, including the youth with his hand on my sleeve, staring at the stairway.

The singing grew louder; it began to echo down the platform behind us, reminding me of my cathedral comparison earlier. How odd, I thought, that such a place could have such wonderful acoustics. That one voice was sounding better and better as it got closer and closer. I knew that whoever the voice belonged to would decide my fate for that night, perhaps for my life.

The miracle is, no one appeared at the top of the stairs. No Irish cop, no late-night reveler, no choir member, no one. The footfalls came to a stop there and the singing voice was instantly drowned out. I was just as disturbed as I was relieved.

What drowned out the voice in those final moments was the approaching roar of my train coming into the station. The platform filled with people, and then a transit cop disembarked. I am sure I was saved because the young men were waiting to discover the identity of the singer with the heavy tread.

I called my mother the next day to tell her about the eerie happening, and she began to cry. She said that the previous night she had asked a special prayer—for me to be surrounded by a legion of angels.

But I knew it wasn't necessary to pray for an entire legion. One with a fine voice and a heavy foot was all I needed.

 ## PRAISE HIM FOR HIS MIGHTY ACTS (AND HIS LESSER ONES, TOO)

Efrem Zimbalist, Jr. as told to Regina Walker McCally

Would you believe four flat tires on one car in one day? Well, listen to this.

Back in 1953 I was planning an easy little trip from my home in Connecticut to Pennsylvania. I had four brand new tires for my car. And that was no ordinary car—it was (and is) the motorized love of my life. It's a 1934 Packard, a tan and chocolate brown beauty, with long sleek lines and highly finished grillwork up front. The top lets down, and there's a sturdy running board on either side of the chassis, which rests on gleaming wire wheels. More about those wheels later.

Life was unsettled for me back at that particular time. Emily McNair, my first wife, had died of cancer. Emily and I had bought that Packard together. It had been an old wreck of a car sold to us by a New Englander with a thick Maine accent.

We had hired a mechanic to restore it, but Emily died before the car was finished. So there I was with our two small children, Nancy, seven, and Efrem III, four. And the Packard.

I withdrew from acting for a while to give myself time to heal, and in the interim I began composing music. I come from a musical family. Mother was a beautiful soprano known on the opera stage as Alma Gluck; and my father, a celebrated violinist and composer, was then director of the Curtis Institute of Music in Philadelphia.

Now *my* first work was going to be performed! It was definitely a thrill, the prospect of going down to Merion, on the Main Line outside of Philadelphia, to hear it presented. I'd written a motet, a choral work sung without instrumental accompaniment. It was based on a sacred text, Psalm 150, an unusual sort of composition for me since I wasn't all that religious. At the time, that is. But I'd put my all into that piece, and it was one of the numbers to be performed on a Sunday afternoon program of religious music by a very distinguished group. My father would be in attendance, too.

The plan that Sunday was for me to drive down to New York, park the Packard, then continue by train to Philadelphia, where I would meet my father. Together we would make the short commute by train to Merion. But if I had known then what awaited me, I might never have ventured out that Sunday. I drove a short distance down Route 202, following the Aspetuck River, then turned off onto Route 37 for a shortcut into New York. There were dark clouds overhead, but the day started off happily.

"Tah, dah, tah, tum, Praise ye the Lord . . . Praise him with the timbrel and dance, dah, dah, dah, dah," I sang, lustily, snatches of my choral work that soon would be magnified by many voices. "Oh, Prai-i-i-se him upo-o-o-on—" *POW*! My left tire. My *new* left tire.

"What in the world?" I exclaimed. "I just *bought* those tires." The flat had come just as I entered the small town of Sherman, Connecticut, and it posed an immediate dilemma for me. There were two spares sitting grandly in the sidewells along the running boards, but they were there mostly for show. They were old and couldn't be trusted. So I ran around trying to find a service station—one open on Sunday. The one I finally found had to call Litchfield, twenty-two miles away, and have a tire delivered.

Well, I figured, *that's okay*. I'd allowed an extra hour and a half traveling time.

Annoyed over the delay but glad that I'd started out early, I drove the Packard back onto the highway. "That tire shouldn't have blown. What bad luck," I brooded. Soon, though, I was humming to myself and fantasizing about the reception I'd get for my motet.

"Praise him with the sound of the trumpet: praise him with the psaltery and harp . . ." *HONK! HONK!* Someone waved at the Packard. (The Packard always gets a lot of attention.)

The dark clouds had now opened up, and rain pelted down. Then I heard a second *Pfffft, flop, flop*. My right rear tire!

"This *can't* be happening!" I said out loud. There I was, in the middle of a downpour on the Saw Mill River Parkway. Straining under the Packard's weight, I began jacking up the car; but the jack broke and splattered me with mud. My temper smoldered.

With good leather shoes sinking in the ooze, I tromped off to find a farmhouse and a phone. A wary woman answered my knock. Through the cracked door, she stared suspiciously at my wet suit, the hair plastered to my forehead, the splotches of mud on my face and clothes.

"Strangers ain't allowed here," she said brusquely. *Slam* went the door. *Click* went the latch. Precious time was lost as I persuaded her through the door to call a service station to come and fix my flat. By this time my head start had eroded.

The tire changed, I was back at the wheel, sitting damply on the leather seat, spinning down the Saw Mill, trying desperately to make up for lost time. And then, the third tire went. The Packard limped into a nearby service station.

Through clenched teeth, I called my father in Philadelphia and told him to go on to the concert without me. I would meet him as soon as I could get there. Dad tried to soothe me, but it was no use.

Back in the car, my blood pressure was boiling. My moment of triumph had been lost, all because of those miserable tires. I no longer puzzled over the oddity of their going flat. I was too infuriated.

And so, when the fourth one blew, I was a dangerous man. I banged shut the door of the Packard. Not even the rain could cool me off. And where was I this time? On the Henry Hudson Parkway. I could *see* the city, but I couldn't get to it. Cars whizzed past, barely missing the Packard, parked precariously on the shoulder just at the end of a curve. No one stopped to help; people only honked and yelled warnings and shook their fists.

But I was too angry to give up. I was going to complete this trip if it killed me! Then I heard it, a *chug-chug-sputter-sputter*, and a jalopy, driven by an old white-haired man, pulled up behind me. Off went the engine, and the man's head slumped against the steering wheel.

Minutes passed, nothing happened. Still seething, I stomped over to the old car and asked gruffly through the window: "Hey, what are you doing here?"

When the old fellow looked up, I caught my breath. I hadn't expected the serene, compassionate gaze that met my angry glare. His face was almost, well, beautiful; and although he must have been near eighty, his eyes seemed ageless.

In a feeble voice, with frequent pauses, he explained, "I'm a little tired, and I thought I'd take a rest."

"A rest!" I yelled. "On the Henry Hudson Parkway?" Could this man be pulling my leg? I wondered. I was beginning to think I was going gaga.

"And what are *you* doing here?" the old man asked in a singsong voice.

"I have a flat tire," I snapped. "In fact, it's my fourth flat tire of the day!"

No reply. Then, after a long wait, he said, "There's a garage a mile and a half down, at the next exit. They'll fix it."

"Don't you understand," I fumed, "I have a flat. I can't drive that far on the rim!" Why, I wondered, was I standing here in the rain talking to this old guy?

After another minute's pause, he asked, "Then why don't *you* fix it?"

I wanted to shake this man until his teeth rattled, I was so mad. "Because my jack broke!" I replied, exasperated by this slow-motion conversation.

Looking at my mud-spattered watch, I realized that the concert would be starting soon.

"I have a jack," said the old man, and he handed me the keys to his trunk.

"Why didn't you say so in the first place?" I said huffily, as I got the jack. As quickly as I could, I changed the tire, then returned the man's jack and keys. Neither of us spoke.

I went back to the Packard, whacked on the hubcap. Then, feeling guilty about my rudeness, I turned back to thank the old gentleman. And I gasped! Jalopy and man had vanished. Without a *sound*. I remembered the sputtering of his engine when he pulled up behind me. There was no way to sneak off in *that* car.

I ran up the Parkway and looked into the distance, cars zooming and screeching around me. No trace of him. "I *am* losing my mind," I said out loud.

Then I began to wonder. Was that man real or wasn't he? The spare tire in place on the front of my car was proof that he'd lent me a jack. But he couldn't have disappeared in those few seconds—twenty at the most—while my back was turned. It was weird. I felt a shiver down my spine.

On the train ride down to Philadelphia, I continued to puzzle over the old man. *Of course*, I thought, *if it hadn't been for him, I'd still be standing helplessly on the Parkway. But on the other hand, he wasn't all that helpful. He didn't do anything, in fact, until I told him point-blank what I needed. And yet, he gave it—a jack, that's all I needed. And then he disappeared. Just* who *was he?*

All those flats, I later found out, occurred because the mechanic failed to put on the boots with the Packard's new tires. The boots would have protected the tires from the Packard's spoked wheels.

But, you know, I never forgot that old man, and years later, when I drew closer to God, I felt—and I believe now—that that old man was sent to help me. As exasperating as he was, he gave me the help I needed. But he made me ask for it.

"Ask, and it shall be given you; seek, and ye shall find." (Matthew 7:7).

But wait, there's more to the story of that day. I walked into the concert in Merion, *two hours* late, just as the choral group burst into "Praise ye the Lord . . . Praise him for his mighty acts . . . " The 150th Psalm—*my* motet! Knowing I was delayed, the conductor pushed it back on the program until he felt he could not hold off any longer; and at that moment, I pushed wearily through the doors.

I sat there, muddy and wet, and listened humbly, as the choir's voice swelled at the end: "Let everything that hath breath praise the Lord. Praise ye the Lord."

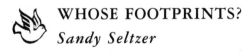 WHOSE FOOTPRINTS?
Sandy Seltzer

Dustin, my California-bred guide dog, was having trouble outside our Long Island apartment. This was his first snowstorm and he was confused. I'm blind, and I wasn't doing so well either. No one was out, so there were no sounds to steer me. Contrary to what many people think, guide dogs do not find the way for a blind person. The blind person directs the dog.

After a harrowing forty-five minutes, Dustin and I finally made it back. But guide dogs must be walked regularly. "Next time why don't you ask God to go with you?" a friend suggested. And so I did. "Lord, go with Dustin and me. The wind is so fierce it's hard to concentrate on our direction. Lead us."

Snow stung our faces and it was difficult to make a path. Dustin whined a little. "Okay, boy," I said to him, "the Lord is with us." And then I gave him a command that a blind person gives only when another person is leading the way: "Dustin, follow!"

Dustin perked up and to my astonishment took off as though he knew exactly where to go. We made it to the street, then headed back to our building—no problem.

A young woman trudged up and offered to walk us to our door. "We'll just follow your footprints," she said. "Yours and the dog's, and that other person's."

"What other person?" I asked.

"There's a dog's prints. And your prints. And a larger person's prints. Wasn't someone with you?"

I paused for a moment and then I answered, "Oh yes, there was Someone with us." There always is.

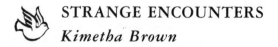

STRANGE ENCOUNTERS
Kimetha Brown

I was exhausted, numb with grief and shock and fear. The last twenty-four hours had been an unceasing nightmare. I didn't see how God could permit such things to happen to anyone, let alone my little boy, David. I didn't know whether he would survive; the doctors said they couldn't tell me. I didn't know whether the mountain lion that had mauled him was rabid or not. I stood in the hospital corridor and turned my face to the wall and wept silent tears of hopelessness and despair.

Then, although I had heard no one come up behind me, I felt a pair of loving arms enfold me—gentle, supportive, understanding arms. I thought it must be my husband, Chris. Or perhaps some friend or relative who had heard about our trouble and had hurried to the hospital.

But it was not my husband. It was not a friend. It was someone I had never seen before.

And would never see again . . .

The unbelievable had happened the previous day on a rocky trail in Big Bend National Park on the Texas side of the Mexican border. It was a scorching afternoon, August 2, 1984. As my two sons, David, eight, and Justin, four, raced ahead of us, their stepfather, Chris, called them back, reminding them that the park rangers had told us to stick together. They had said that these piñon-juniper woodlands hid coyote, white-tailed deer, javelina, desert mule, even some mountain lions that occasionally were seen at a distance. But no one had ever been threatened by these. The thing to watch out for on the path we were taking, they said, was snakes.

Suddenly, David swung around, his face contorted with fear. He ran toward us screaming, "Mountain lion!"

Before any of us could react, a cougar sprang from the shadow of a tree. Like a tawny streak of lightning it pounced on David's back. The next moment he lay sprawled, not moving, as the huge cat clamped its teeth over his head . . .

There are moments in life that burn themselves into your brain, into your soul. That moment burned into mine. As I stood there in the hospital corridor, I knew it would never go away. And yet, as the gentle arms enfolded me, a soft voice said, "Child, you don't know me. But I know you." I turned and found myself gazing into the face of an elderly black man. He was wearing dark glasses. He wore some kind of old hat. He held a small brown paper bag in one hand, the top crumpled shut. I think—but I'm not absolutely sure of this—he was wearing some sort of brown coveralls.

All this I saw through my tears at a glance. My first reaction was one of astonishment, resistance, almost fright. He must have felt me

stiffen, because he said soothingly, "I know all about you and why you
are here. God knows too."

I heard these words with incredulity. How could he know about me?
No newspaper had published the story. There hadn't been time. And
yet, startled and incredulous though I was, I was aware that something
remarkable was happening. I have a normal wariness of strangers, but
in an instant, it seemed, something melted away that resistance. I no
longer felt afraid. I just felt loved. I yielded to the comfort of this
stranger's arms. And cried . . .

When the cougar pounced, I watched in horror, unable to
move or make a sound. But Chris burst into action. He hurled
himself at the lion, trying to kick it away from David. The
beast writhed in pain and anger, but did not release its hold on
the child. Chris slipped and fell almost on top of them. I
screamed, "He's killing him! He's killing him!" Chris seized
the cougar by the neck, trying to choke it. Justin was running
in circles like a mad thing. When I snatched him to me, he
climbed all over me, half crazed with fear. I wanted to calm
him, but I couldn't stop screaming.

With colossal effort, Chris wrenched the cougar away from
David and flung it aside, but the enraged beast came right
back, sinking its claws into his leg. With his free foot, Chris
kicked with all his might and the cougar flew backward. Chris
snatched up a tiny stick and lunged at the lion with a furious
yell. The bluff—and what a courageous bluff it was—worked.
The animal sprang into the underbrush and disappeared.

Chris scooped David up in his arms. David's eyes were open
but filled with blood. His skull lay exposed; parts of his scalp
hung in shreds, bleeding terribly. There were tooth and claw
marks all over the upper part of his body. But he was alive.

"Got to stay together!" Chris gasped at me. "Thing might
come back!" He tried to hoist David onto his back, but our son
was too weak to hold on. So Chris carried him in his arms. After
about fifty yards he stopped long enough to rip off his shirt and
wrap it tightly around David's head. Then we ran together back
toward the lodge and help. But it was more than half an hour
away. I didn't see how Chris could make it with a seventy-two-
pound load of dead weight in his arms. Twice I saw the bushes
move on the side of the path. The lion was trailing us.

"Daddy," David murmured weakly, "am I going to die?"

"No, you're not!" Chris assured him. "We're going to pray."
And as we stumbled on, we did pray. Chris thanked God for
sparing David's life. He asked for healing for David, and for
strength for himself to make it back to the lodge. David joined
in, and as they prayed together I saw blood running down
Chris's leg. I couldn't tell if it was David's blood or my
husband's. They both ran together. A short while later, I
remembered a phrase from the Bible where another David said,
"The Lord delivered me from the paw of the lion" (1 Samuel
17:37). I clung to that . . .

*I clung to it just as I was clinging now to my comforting stranger.
He said, "God sent me to tell you that your little boy will be restored."
Restored. What a strange, archaic word, but one with such healing
power in it. And hadn't that other David also used that word in the
loveliest of his songs, "He restoreth my soul . . ."? My own soul was
being restored. The fear and despair were leaving me.*

*Now the old man whose arms held me so securely began to pray in a
low, musical voice, the most beautiful prayer I ever expect to hear this
side of Heaven. He thanked God for saving David's life. He thanked
Him for giving Chris and me the strength we needed. Listening to him,
I was sure that God was listening too. I knew that David was going to
be all right . . .*

When at last we stumbled into the lodge, the horrified
rangers sprang into action. A paramedic treated David's terrible
wounds as best he could. An old park van rushed him to the
nearest hospital in the small town of Alpine 110 miles away.
We prayed together the whole way. There nurses tried to clean
and dress the wounds according to instructions given over the
telephone by a trauma team at the Parkland Hospital in Dallas.
It was imperative that David be rushed to Parkland for spe-
cialized care. The danger was that the exposed skull might dry
out and "die," and thus the brain could be affected.

We tried to get an airplane for the five-hundred-mile trip,
but ran into nothing but delays and frustrations. Finally in
desperation we left in the middle of the night by ambulance and
didn't get to Dallas till the next morning. By then David was
running a fever; the antibiotics he had received didn't seem to
be controlling the infection that had set in. Meanwhile, heli-

copters and dogs were out tracking the cougar. To be safe, David had to begin the painful series of rabies shots on top of everything else. It seemed more than an eight-year-old body should have to endure . . .

The old man stepped back, his hand still on my arm, and I knew he was about to go. I wanted to ask his name, know how he knew about David, how he knew about our need. But he shook his head and smiled as I formed the first question. "I want you to look at my eyes," he said. He took off the dark glasses. His eyes were white. He was completely blind. "I wanted you to see this," he said, "so that you would understand that God really did send me. Watch!"

He turned and walked unerringly down the long, busy hospital corridor. Straight as an arrow, with no cane to guide him, without touching the walls on either side. He did not bump into anyone or anything. I watched him go, the old hat still on his head, the brown paper bag still clutched in his right hand. He turned a corner and was gone. I never saw him again. And even though I asked around, no one in the hospital knew him—or had even seen him.

Today, a year later, David is almost healed, physically and psychologically. He still has occasional nightmares, but they're less frequent. Two more skin grafts are needed, but his hair has almost covered his scalp now. Doctors are amazed by the rapid progress he is making.

They tracked down the cougar. Small amounts of David's hair and skin were in its stomach, positively identifying it. Surprisingly, tests showed no signs of rabies. No one can guess what made this two-year-old female lion attack. In the fifty years the park has been open, such a thing had never happened before.

And that meeting in the Parkland corridor? If you are invincibly literal-minded I suppose you can choose to believe that the person I met — or the person who came to me — was just some casual visitor to the hospital who had heard about David, and who was remarkably perceptive and kind.

But Chris and I will never believe that. We believe that God heard our prayers and sent one of His messengers, yes, a blind messenger with a funny hat and a brown paper bag, to comfort and strengthen us. We'll believe it forever. And we'll never cease to be thankful.

THE FAR SIDE OF MIDNIGHT
Irene J. Kutz

From the time I was a child my parents taught me to believe in God and to know Him. But as I grew up I learned that knowing God and being a professional Christian do not always keep difficulties or heartbreak away. Indeed, there was one time in my life when I felt that God had deserted me altogether.

It happened during World War II, when I was only twenty. Allen was twenty-one. He was in the artillery, the Timberwolf division. He was a Christian, too, and we pledged our lives together and our love to God.

When Allen went overseas with his division, a part of him stayed with me. We were to be married when he returned. We prayed for an early end to the war.

But then there was the Battle of the Bulge. Allen did not come through it.

Words cannot express the agony I felt. From the beginning, from the first time we met, our lives had been so intertwined I had felt that there could be no life for me if his ceased. I could not see how a loving God could permit such sorrow to come to me.

The night I learned of Allen's death was one of heavy, gloomy rain. Unable to talk to anyone, I put on my slicker and hat, and went out to walk in the downpour, trying to escape the unbearable loss, the despair. But they stayed with me.

I don't know how long I walked, or where I went, but finally I found myself on the bridge over the river that flowed through our town, an old-fashioned drawbridge with a bridge-tender who stayed in a little house on the main span, raising the center section when boats came by. I knew he was there, but I was sure that he would not be able to see me in the darkness and the rain.

I leaned over the railing and gazed down into the churning water below, just barely visible by the lights of the town. I had always lived for God, trying to do His will, and now He had betrayed me. If I could just slip over the side into the dark water, oh, the blissful oblivion, the release from pain. The agony of drowning would be over in moments—nothing compared to the torment now tearing me apart. *Oh, Allen,* I thought, *Allen, Allen . . .*

I heard no sound, but suddenly I felt a hand on my arm. "Come in out of the rain," the bridge-tender said quietly. Numbly I let him lead me to his tiny house on the bridge. He sat me down on one of the two chairs, and poured a cup of coffee from his thermos. Pain possessed me, consumed me. I felt as if I *were* pain.

"It's a nasty night to be out," he remarked. He had removed his slicker, and I did not recognize him as one of the regular men. He was a little man, with an ageless face, and his eyes— the bluest, deepest-set I had ever seen—were compassionate and kind. I had never seen him before, but I felt his spirit touching mine.

I began to cry, and he sat there, across the little table from me, saying nothing. Oddly, his silence didn't seem strange to me; he did not seem like a stranger.

A boat's whistle hooted three times down the river. The man set in motion the huge mechanism that raised the bridge. The boat passed through, and the bridge settled back into place.

My sobbing had quieted, and I found myself telling him about Allen, spilling out my soul as if I'd known him all my life. When I finished, I felt drained, exhausted, but the unbearable knife-edge sharpness was gone.

His eyes stayed on my face as he said quietly, "I can understand your grief." Then he took both my hands in his. "Father," he murmured, "come to Your child."

He bowed his head in silent prayer for several minutes. Then he raised it. "Come now. I'll walk with you to the end of the bridge. The Lord will see you through this. Remember that."

I walked home. I still grieved, but the awful despair was alleviated. I knew somehow that God had not forsaken me. I felt I was no longer alone.

Several days later, I walked down to the river to tell the bridge-tender that I was slowly learning to live with my loss, and to thank him. But he wasn't there.

I described him to the man on duty.

"I don't know who you're talking about, Miss, and I know all the tenders," he told me.

"But the night it rained so hard . . ." I persisted.

"I'm sorry. I don't know who was on duty that night."
I never found out who that man was, and I know I never will.
But I do know Who sent him to me.

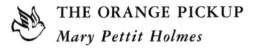

THE ORANGE PICKUP
Mary Pettit Holmes

I had to stay late that evening at the bloodmobile, where I am a
registered nurse working with the American Red Cross. By the
time I trudged out to my car, it was dark, and fog was rolling
in. I had an hour's drive home to our small town nestled near
the base of the Oregon coastal range.

The traffic was light, which was good, because the fog was
getting heavier. I could barely see the white line at the edge of
the freeway and the streetlamps that lit it. Then I turned off
onto our country road. Ten more miles to drive on a narrow,
twisting road with deep ditches and a stream alongside.

"Help me, Lord," I prayed. Recently in church we had been
discussing the use of mental imaging while praying. Now I
visualized Jesus sitting next to me in the passenger seat. I
poured out my fears to Him.

Hugging the steering wheel, I stared at the eerie whiteness.
Suddenly ahead of me I saw the red taillights of another car.
Slowly I drew closer. The red taillights were on an orange
pickup being hauled by a tow truck. I was relieved. Undoubt-
edly the pickup was being taken to the garage in Forest Grove.
If I followed it, I could make it home.

We came to Main Street—but we passed the repair shop. The
tow truck drove on. It kept going. To my amazement, it turned
into the dead-end road where we lived. With a sigh of relief I
turned into our driveway, then quickly got out to thank the
driver of the tow truck that had led me home.

There was no driver. There was no tow truck. It had not
turned around to exit from the dead end. I stood staring into the
silent fog at the end of our road.

THE MAN IN THE TREE
Delta Ralls

"Wake up! Water's rising fast!" Somebody was pounding hard on the door of our camper.

When my husband, Earl, and I first fell asleep, rain was hammering on our metal roof like machine-gun fire. Now it was pretty close to midnight, and a ranger outside was hollering that people should move their boats in to shelter.

It was Wednesday, May 27, 1987, and we'd been fishing and camping with some relatives at Chisholm Trail Ridge on Waurika Lake, about twelve miles from where we lived in Comanche, Oklahoma.

By the time I pulled on my jogging pants, Earl had disappeared into the downpour. But in a minute he came back, holding up half a boat key. "Broke off in the ignition," he yelled.

"I'll go for the spare," I yelled back. We had another key at home, and it seemed easy enough to go get it.

I climbed into our yellow pickup and took off, the windshield wipers flapping away but not helping much. I followed the road along the shore, the pickup bouncing over the ruts. Lightning flashed, and in the eerie blue-white light, trees were bent over and the tall grass was almost flattened by the wind.

I pulled into our driveway, grabbed up the boat key, and headed back around the lake, past Beaver Creek bottom.

By now the storm was even worse. I jounced along over potholes, hoping I was still on the road, when . . .

The pickup lurched, then reeled out of control. Something smashed into the pickup and sent it hurtling through the air. I held on to the steering wheel as hard as I could. Then the pickup dropped with a thud. Icy water poured in everywhere. I threw myself against the door, pushed it open, and fell into churning water that sucked me into the darkness.

Lord help me. I can't swim. I couldn't get my breath. Water stung my eyes, my nose, my throat. I flailed desperately for something, anything, to hold on to.

The water roared like a freight train in a tunnel.

A tree branch! I grabbed it with both hands. The force of the water whipped me around the tree, but I held on. I wrapped my legs around the tree trunk and groped in the darkness for a branch strong enough to climb onto. There! A branch! I hauled myself up and clung to it, shaking.

This couldn't be happening to me—alone. I wanted to cry out for Earl.

Earl! I loved my husband—and totally relied on him. I always had, ever since I came home from the first grade in a one-room schoolhouse in Sugden, Oklahoma, and told Mama I'd be marrying Earl Ralls. Ever since then, when things went wrong, Earl was beside me. I was shy and scared of folks, so Earl always took care of things, protected me.

This time it was just me. And God.

But what a time finally to be thinking of God: when I was in trouble! Why hadn't I been a better Christian? My faith had never wavered, but over the past five years my church attendance hadn't been too regular.

I figured if you were fifty-one years old, unable to swim, sitting in a tree in the middle of the night during a flood, you'd better be prayed up.

I wasn't.

Would God hear me anyhow? I bowed my head against the driving rain and asked for His help.

There was nothing to do now except hold tight and wait. But the rushing water was creeping over my feet and up my legs.

When I was ten, a bunch of us kids were on the lake holding on to the back of a boat, when I got a cramp and had to let go. I'll never forget that feeling of terror as water filled my nose and throat. But Earl's strong arm pulled me out of the water and saved my life. I never did learn to swim, but I learned I could always depend on Earl Ralls.

But Earl wasn't here to tell me what to do in this darkness. Panic-stricken, I reached up for a limb above me . . .

"Don't climb higher until morning."

Was I hearing things? Where did those words come from? I was too terrified to question. I sank back and huddled against the trunk of the tree.

Hour after hour, I held on while the flood roared around me. Gradually light filtered through black clouds. Morning. The water was up to my waist.

I looked up. The branch I'd reached for in the night was

dead. It would have cracked under my weight. The strange command I'd heard last night had kept me from falling into the swirling black water. *God, thank You.*

This time I tested each branch beforehand. Little by little I climbed higher. I scanned the horizon for a boat, rooftop, or any sign of life. But only treetops swayed in the rushing flood. There was no sign of my pickup. I opened my mouth to scream for help.

"Save your strength. Don't yell unless you hear something."

Was someone really speaking to me? Or was I imagining those words? I clung to the tree silently.

More hours went by. By now I was desperately thirsty. I tried to sip a handful of the water surging around me, but the flood had washed manure-spotted pastures, flushed out septic tanks, and carried off the carcasses of dead animals. I gagged.

"Lord," I said out loud, "I'm thirsty."

"Suck your shirt."

I looked around in astonishment. And then down at my T-shirt. I lowered my head, gathered the fabric into my mouth, and sucked out fresh rainwater.

The light faded and the temperature dropped. Thursday evening! Could I stand another night shivering in the darkness? Could I stay awake? Or be able to hold on? My fingers were raw and bloody from clutching the rough bark. I was exhausted, limp, and weak. But worst of all, I was lonely.

I blinked, then blinked again.

Sitting on the branch across from me was the largest man I'd ever seen.

I shut my eyes tight, then opened them slowly.

He was still there. Even in the gathering dusk, I could see his eyes clearly. They were incredibly kind.

Neither of us said a word. His presence radiated warmth and comfort. My shivering stopped; I was enveloped in a cocoon of peace. It was like being in a chapel. For the first time, I relaxed and rested.

The hours passed.

At last the man spoke. His voice was gentle but full of authority. "I'm leaving now," he said. "Don't be afraid; I'm going to bring help."

"Don't go!" I begged. "The water's too rough."

"I'm strong," he said. "Don't worry. Everything will be all right."

He disappeared into the darkness as suddenly as he had come. Soon it was close to dawn. A bone-chilling wind blew up and whipped the rain into a stinging spray. "Lord, I'm so cold!" I said. And at that moment my body warmed. I felt as though I were being enveloped in a soft, warm blanket. I could almost touch it. I stared at my bare arms in astonishment. There was nothing over them. And yet I actually felt cozy, and my shivering stopped.

Friday morning. I couldn't believe I was still holding on. But who was ever going to find me here? Where was the mysterious man? He hadn't come back.

In a flash it hit me. That man wasn't human! But I knew I hadn't imagined him. He'd been there, talked to me. "I'm going to bring help," he had said.

Could he have been an angel? I'd read about them in the Bible. They were called messengers.

But now I was getting weaker. I couldn't hold on much longer. The water was up to my waist again and still rising. I climbed the last few feet to the top of the tree. Then came the voice again.

"Call for help now."

By now I didn't even wonder if it was real or not. "Help!" I shouted as loud as I could. My voice cracked. "Help!"

Only silence. The water was creeping past my waist now, up and up.

Death. So this was it. Then why wasn't I afraid? All I could think of was the warm blanket that had covered me during the night, and the stranger who had brought me such peace. I closed my eyes.

Voices! Voices not there right beside me but away in the distance. Voices coming closer and closer. I screamed with all my might.

"Wave!" someone out there called. "Wave so we can see you!"

Out of the haze came a small boat rowed by two men.

I woke up between clean white hospital sheets at Duncan Regional Hospital with Earl sitting right beside me, smiling and holding my hand hard. The rest of my family was there too, and Bob Waitman, pastor of the Patterson Avenue Baptist Church. They told me dozens of people had been over at the church praying that I'd be safe.

Earl and the others had been searching around the Dry Creek bottomland, but I'd been much farther to the west. "You were close to the Youngblood place," Earl told me. "The Youngblood kids went looking for their missing horse and found it in an orchard feeding on some peaches. You must have yelled at just the right moment, because they heard you and ran home, and Mrs. Youngblood radioed for help."

A nurse was turning away folks who had flocked to see me. Earl had told her how shy and scared of people I was, so everybody was surprised when I sat up and said, "Let them in!"

People I'd known all my life, and people I'd never spoken to, put their arms around me; some of them cried. Everybody was amazed at how well I had held up. But I told them, "Don't be thinking I'm Superwoman at fifty-one years of age! The Lord was with me."

For certain, the Lord *had* been with me. And so had that mysterious man. I didn't tell anyone about him then, yet I believe he was an angel.

I'm not so scared of being "out in the world" now. I have a kind of confidence and trust that I didn't have before.

Because I know now that God is always there when I need Him.

His arm is even longer than Earl's.

A Note to the Reader

His Mysterious Ways, Volume II, is published by the same people who publish *Guideposts*—a monthly magazine filled with true stories of people's adventures in faith.

If you have found inspiration in this book, we think you'll find help and inspiration in the stories that appear in our magazine.

Guideposts is not sold on the newsstand. It's available by subscription only. And subscribing is easy. All you have to do is write Guideposts Associates, Inc., 39 Seminary Hill Road, Carmel, New York, 10512. For those with special reading needs, *Guideposts* is also published in Big Print, Braille, and Talking Magazine.

When you subscribe, each month you can count on receiving exciting new evidence of God's presence and His abiding love for His people.